IMAGES
of America

HOBOKEN

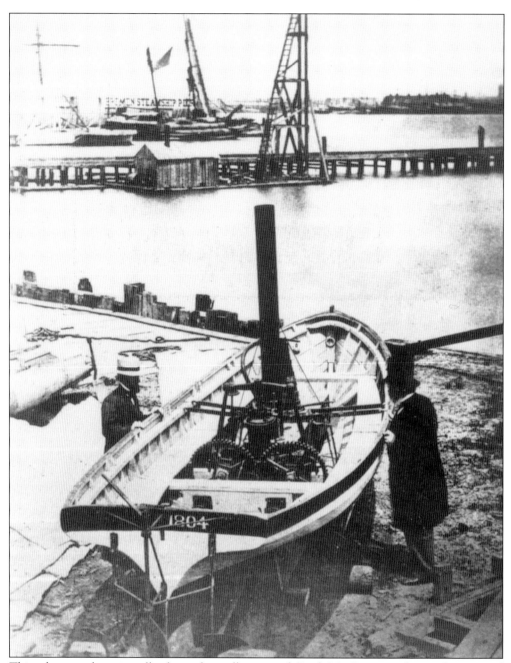

This photograph, originally from the collection of Basil M. Stevens, shows the original twin-screw engine and boiler built in Hoboken in 1804, by Stevens's grandfather, the inventor Colonel John Stevens. The Hoboken Ferry Company exhibited this engine at the 1892 Columbian Exhibition in Chicago. (Courtesy of the Hoboken Public Library.)

Cover Image: In this view of Hoboken Terminal, looking west toward the rail yard, light filters through the Bush Trail Sheds. Lincoln Bush was chief engineer for the railroad from 1902 to 1909. (William B. Barry, photographer, DL&W Collection, Syracuse University.)

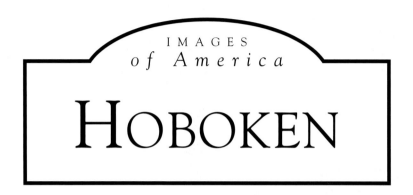

IMAGES
of America

HOBOKEN

Patricia Florio Colrick

ARCADIA
PUBLISHING

Copyright © 1999 by Patricia Florio Colrick
ISBN 978-0-7385-3730-6

Published by Arcadia Publishing,
Charleston SC, Chicago IL, Portsmouth NH, San Francisco CA

Printed in the United States of America

Library of Congress Catalog Card Number: 2004114115

For all general information, contact Arcadia Publishing:
Telephone 843-853-2070
Fax 843-853-0044
E-mail sales@arcadiapublishing.com
For customer service and orders:
Toll-free 1-888-313-2665

Visit us on the Internet at www.arcadiapublishing.com

CONTENTS

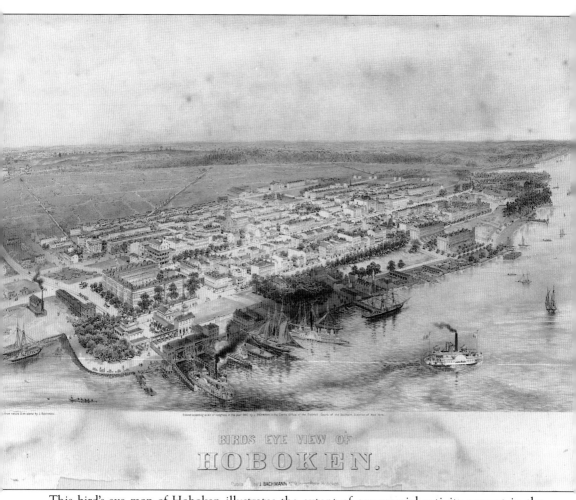

BIRDS EYE VIEW OF

HOBOKEN.

Pub. by J. BACHMANN N° 9 Barclay St. Hoboken

This bird's-eye map of Hoboken illustrates the extent of commercial activity present in the terminal area in 1860. John Bachmann created the map from meticulous observation of the buildings and topography. Hoboken was laid out in a grid pattern in 1804, on the Loss Map by the inventor and owner of much of the land, Colonel John Stevens. The area to the west of the city is seen in its unimproved state, marshland drained by a creek. The commercial activity in this map is centered on the ferry and rail terminal (lower left). The easternmost block at the time was Hudson Street, which was edged to its south and along the river with trees. Residential blocks had been laid out by this time, many of which were block-square groupings of Gothic and Greek Revival structures. The waterfront area had both transportation and commercial usage, with a rustically landscaped area known as Elysian Fields (Fields of Paradise), beginning at the foot of Fourth Street and running northward along the riverfront. John Bachmann (active 1850–1877) resided at 9 Irving Place, a grouping of 14 houses that was completed by 1852 on the west side of Garden Street between Fifth and Sixth Streets. (Stevens Family Papers Collection, New Jersey Historical Commission.)

INTRODUCTION

The City of Hoboken has fascinated me for many years before I ever researched its rich history. As a commuter, I would often opt to take the bus into Manhattan instead of the PATH trains so that I could view, through its windows, the blocks of 19th- and early-20th-century homes and businesses along Washington Street. The concentration of houses, the infinite diversity found in the mason's and carpenter's craft, as well as the religious and commercial landmarks abounding throughout the area were very impressive. Years later, after completing graduate studies in historic preservation and working with the New York Landmarks Conservancy, it was my honor to work as a preservationist with Hoboken's Community Development Agency. This was shortly after the city had established a historic district in the downtown area and a time when the storefront rehabilitation program was in full swing. Living and working in Hoboken in the early 1980s gave me a good foundation for appreciating the challenges facing Hoboken as redevelopment and change loomed in its future. Upon returning to Hoboken after several years, it has been encouraging to see how much has been preserved and that the city continues to be well cared for and appreciated. The Hoboken Historical Museum, founded by Jim Hans in 1986, will be establishing a permanent exhibit space in the Shipyard Development at Hudson Street. The Historical Museum carries out an admirable program of changing exhibits and events, as well as publishing a newsletter and magazine. For membership information, contact PO Box 707, Hoboken, NJ 07030. The Hoboken Fire Department Museum, a site on the National Register, is located at 215 Bloomfield Avenue and is open most Saturdays. Its displays relate the exciting history of the firefighters of Hoboken through historic photographs, apparatus, and other memorabilia. Another recommended stop is Hoboken's Police Department display, featuring artifacts and memorabilia relating to the Police Department, which can be found at the Police Department Headquarters on Hudson Street. Also at this writing, the waiting room and train concourse of the Lackawanna Terminal are undergoing a major preservation effort that will return the magnificent space to its former glory.

Several volumes would be required to document the long and fascinating history of the city of Hoboken. Many 19th-century publications about Hoboken list the history of the Stevens family, the ferryboat advancements, and Stevens Institute of Technology. *The Hoboken of Yesterday* by George Long Moller (1964) and *The Bicentennial History of Hoboken* by John Heaney offer comprehensive looks at the progress of the city through the Stevens family as well as individual religious institutions, clubs, and schools. This book attempts, through historic photographs, to relate the story of the growth of the city and the changes that have occurred there over time. Some of the most noteworthy landmarks of architecture and transportation history are noted, and changes to the waterfront from the late 19th to early 20th century are explored. Of particular note are the photographs of the Elysian Camera Club, in a well-organized archive at the Hoboken Public Library. The club, founded in 1902, was a member of the Associated Camera Clubs of America. Equipment for photographic processing and the making of lantern slides was located at the club's headquarters at 307 Washington Street. Through the efforts of librarian Mrs. Nina Hatfield in 1933, an exhibit of photographs of Hoboken was held and prints subsequently donated, forming the bulk of the Hoboken Public Library's picture collection. The collection was further enhanced by a grant from the State of New Jersey Department of Education Maintenance and Preservation of Library Collections and the Friends of the Hoboken Public Library. This grant enabled the collection to be indexed by Jim Hans and its photographs reproduced. The collection is a resource of great importance.

I would like to acknowledge the encouragement and assistance of the following individuals during this project. Professor Benedict J. Fernandez, the former chairman of the Department of Photography at the New University of New York (currently professor at LaGuardia College and Parsons School of Design) as well as the contributing professor at the Corcoran Gallery in Washington, D.C., has made available to me prints made from original photographs in the collection of the family of Carl J. Willenborg Jr. Mr. Willenborg was his former Garden Street neighbor and longtime Hoboken resident. The Willenborg family shared a friendship with the western artist and Hoboken resident Charles Schreyvogel. The photographic newsletter, *Hoboken Almanac*, is published by Professor Fernandez at 1252 Garden Street, Hoboken, NJ 07030. The North Jersey Electric Railway Historical Society, through its president, Robert E. Hooper, has kindly provided several unusual views of Hoboken and its transportation history for inclusion in this book. The Ira Deutsch Collection, which features record photographs of terminals, equipment, and maintenance, is a unique resource. For information on membership, contact the North Jersey Electric Railway Historical Society, Box 1770, Rahway, NJ 07065. I am also grateful to railroad historians John Willever and Wes Coates, Terry Sasso and the staff of the Hoboken Public Library, especially Senior Reference Librarian Mark Sannino; to the historians Jim Hans, George Kirchgessner, and Hoboken Historical Museum President Leonard Luizzi and Secretary Marie Luizzi; to Ed Shirak Jr., author of the 1995 book, *Our Way in Honor of Frank Sinatra* (available at his retail confectionary store, Lepore's, 537 Garden St., Hoboken), and chair of the November 1999 Hostra University Cultural Center's conference, "The Man, the Music, and the Legend," for his assistance; to Dorothy Unruth Bloodgood, Randy Gabrielan, Al Mankoff, and Patricia Politis for loaning materials; to John Williams and Barbara Hall of the Hagley Museum and Library; *Ticonderoga* curator Chip Stulen and Robyn Woodworth of the Shelburne Museum; Carolyn Davis at the Syracuse University Library Special Collections Department; Ann B. Whiteside of Harvard University; Frank Smolar and Peter Saklas of New Jersey Transit; Nydia Cruz of Stevens Institute of Technology Samuel Williams Library; Dr. Charles Wrege, Professor at Cornell University and Professor Emeritus, Rutgers University, Lance Metz, Historian, National Canal Museum, Easton, PA, and Norman Brower, Librarian, South Street Seaport Museum; David Miller, Duquesne Heights Incline (at 1220 Grandview Avenue in Pittsburgh), the site of a preserved and functioning "incline plane" and traction museum; for research guidance, thanks to the librarians of the Ellis Island Foundation; John Maxtone-Graham, president of the Ocean Liner Museum, who shared photographs of the *Imperator* that were gathered from his research of the HAPAG archives in Germany. Mr. Maxtone-Graham's books, *Crossing and Cruising* and *The Only Way to Cross*, comprehensively document the broad spectrum of transatlantic travel. For information of the Ocean Liner Museum, contact (212) 717-6251. I would also like to acknowledge the many books and articles by Hoboken-born William Miller; Ed Risky and Richard MacAleer for historical information; and the photographer Steve Zane for his documentary copy photography and images of the city hall safe panels. I was most honored that Mrs. Julia Pratt graciously allowed the inclusion of her late husband Charles Pratt's atmospheric photographs of Hoboken Terminal and ferryboat to appear in this book. To that end, the efforts of photographer John Gossage were also very much appreciated.

It is my hope that the reader will find this book useful in understanding the vast mosaic that comprises the history of Hoboken. The old trolley and horse car right-of-ways, remaining as they do in fragments, and the many surviving landmarks, are evidence of the paths of commerce and growth of the city's neighborhoods.

One

TO THE RIVER BY RAIL AND STEAM

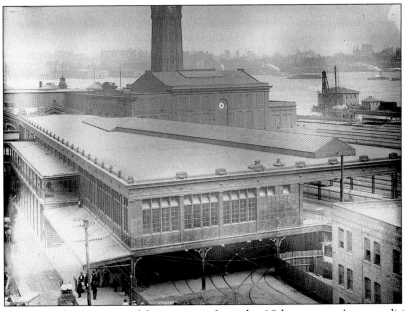

Hoboken has been the location of ferry service from the 18th century. As a condition of its leasing of the land, the railroad was required to link its tracks to the existing ferry service, directed by the Hoboken Land & Improvement Company until 1903. Eventually trolley services also became part of the transportation complex. Today's terminal is the fifth and grandest to occupy the southern tip of Hoboken, and it is actually built on man-made land extensions with its ferry slips located over the water. This bird's-eye view, dating from July of 1910, shows the terminal with all its components (ferry, rail, trolley, and subway) intact. In the foreground is the Public Service Trolley Company's terminal. (Ira Deutsch Collection, North Jersey Electric Railway Historical Society.)

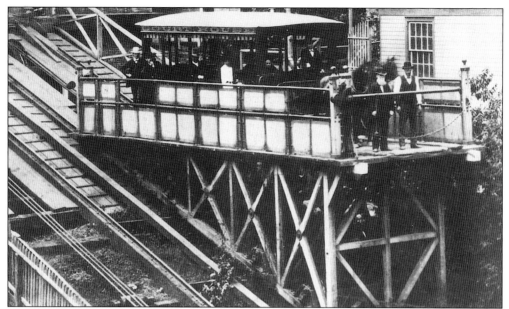

The formidable heights of the Palisades, which separated Jersey City from Hoboken, were overcome by a technological innovation in 1873, when the North Hudson Railway built this incline plane. It was capable of lifting a fully loaded wagon and team up or down the 200-foot distance in one minute. The cable-operated lift was operated by a counterbalanced steam engine, designed by Samuel Diescher of Pittsburgh. (The Duquesne Incline Museum, Pittsburgh.)

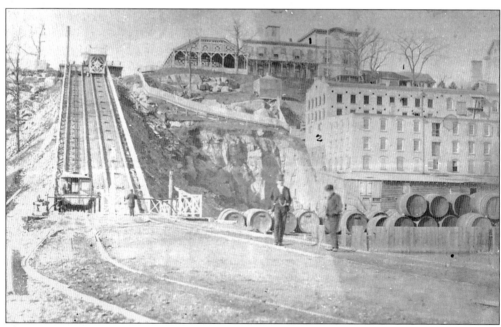

This view, looking up the hill to Jersey City Heights, was taken at the foot of the incline plane wagon elevator. The barrels to the right may be from a local cooperage. Numbered on the photograph are #1 Pohlman's resort and picnic area and #2 Leicht's Brewery. (Courtesy Hoboken Public Library.)

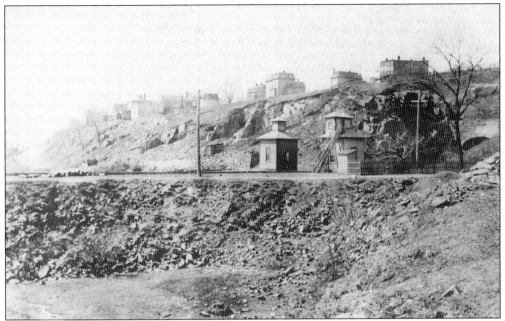

This photograph was taken shortly after the May 12, 1877 completion date of the tracks of the Delaware, Lackawanna, & Western (DL&W) Railroad's Morris and Essex Division. This division replaced the Camden & Amboy Railroad's narrow gauge and connected Hoboken Terminal with points west. (Courtesy Hoboken Public Library.)

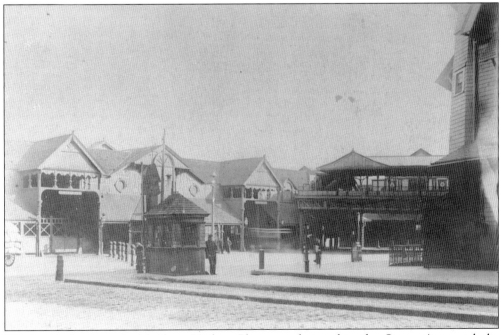

The fourth ferry terminal built at Hudson Place was designed in the Queen Anne style by H. Edwards Ficken in 1883. This postcard view shows the pedestrian and team gateways for the Christopher and Barclay Street ferries. The rail terminal was joined by a roofed passageway to the ferryhouse. (Courtesy Hoboken Public Library.)

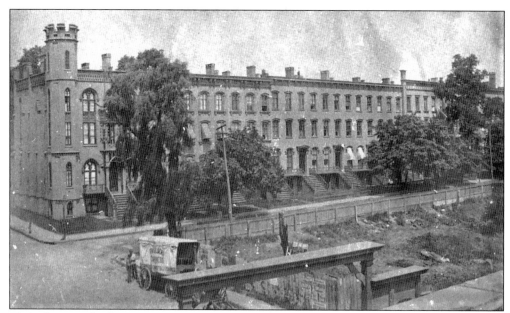

This photograph illustrates the southeastern portion of the Franklin Terrace houses. These substantial structures were designed in the Gothic Revival style in symmetrically arranged sequences to lend diversity to the streetscape. The buildings were coated in a brownstone-like mineral coating developed by Stevens. (Courtesy Hoboken Public Library.)

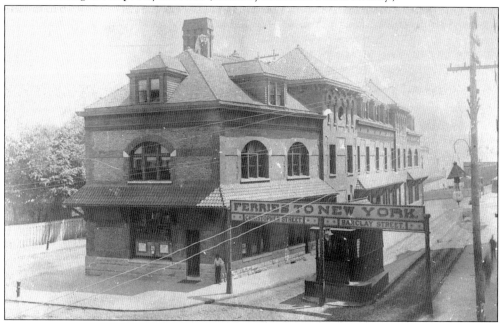

In 1886, H. Edwards Ficken designed a new building for the Hoboken Land & Improvement Company. This corporation directed real estate, commerce, and ferry services in Hoboken from 1838 to 1947. This handsome building was located between the ferryhouse and River Street. The brick and stone-trimmed building was tapered at its corners and was bound on its northern and southern sides to a private cobblestone cartway, which led to ferry thoroughfares. The building's interior lobby design was modeled after that of a ferryboat. (Courtesy Hoboken Public Library.)

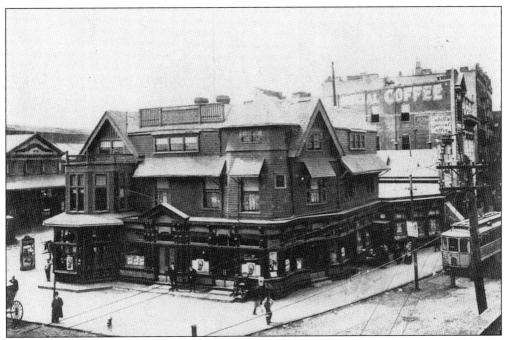

Duke's House, a popular restaurant and bar, was owned by Milton Daab. It was located at the easternmost end of Hudson Place, on the northeast corner. In this photograph, one can see the While Line trolley passing to the north. A section of the trolley terminal can be seen to the left of the c. 1890 photograph. (Courtesy Hoboken Public Library.)

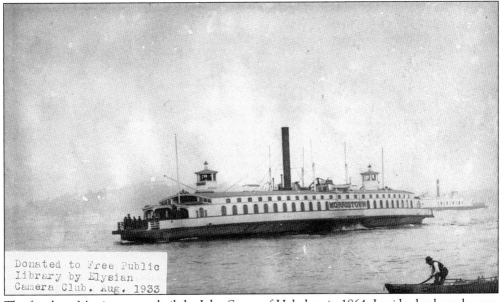

The ferryboat *Morristown* was built by John Stuart of Hoboken in 1864. Its sidewheel can be seen just under the boat's name, to the right of center of the boat. (Courtesy Hoboken Public Library.)

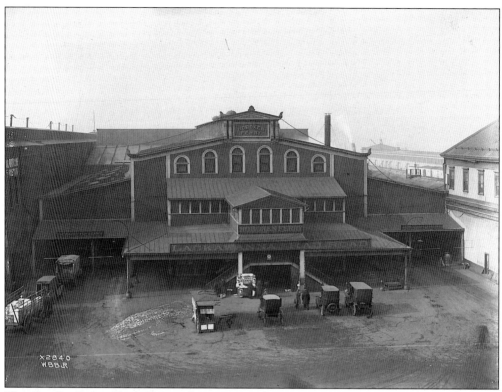

The Barclay Street Ferry Terminal in New York was in use from 1888 to 1967. (DL&W Collection, Syracuse University.)

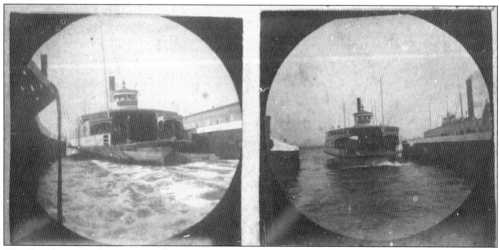

The ferryboats *Lackawanna* and *Bergen* are seen from the interior of the Hoboken ferryhouse in photographs dated October 1889. (Courtesy Hoboken Public Library.)

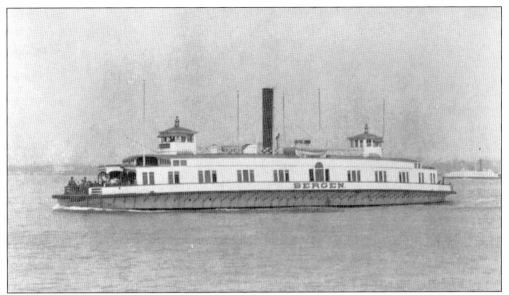

The *Bergen* was the first double-screw ferryboat in the world. Launched in 1888, it was designed by the Hoboken Ferry Company, with an engine designed by J. Shields Wilson of Philadelphia. (Published photograph from *Romance of the Hoboken Ferry*, 1931, courtesy Hoboken Public Library.)

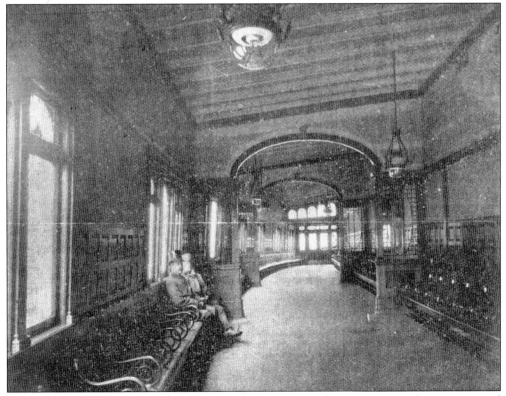

This published photograph of the interior of the ferry *Bergen* shows the commodious seating and generous proportions of the interior. (Courtesy Hoboken Public Library.)

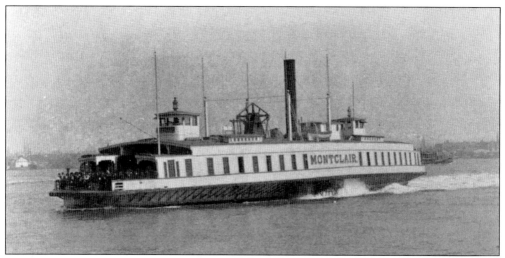

The ferryboats *Montclair* and *Orange* were the last of the sidewheel boats to be built for the Hoboken ferries. The *Montclair* was built in 1886, at Newburgh, New York, and was designed by Francis B. Stevens. (Published photograph from the *Romance of the Hoboken Ferry*, courtesy Hoboken Public Library.)

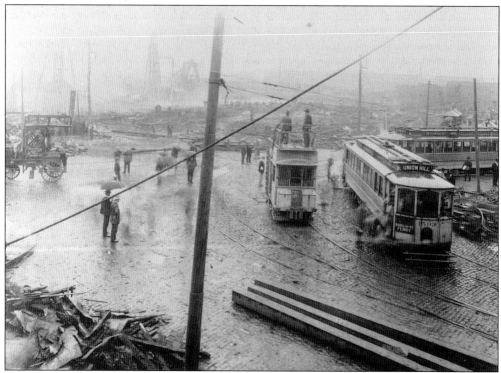

Shortly after 10 p.m. on August 7, 1905, a fire was detected on the upper deck of the ferryboat *Hopatcong*. The fire spread to the *Binghamton* and thence throughout the ferry terminal. By daybreak, both the entire rail and ferry terminal were destroyed. The Immigration Station and Pullman Building (to the south of the terminal), which had been opened earlier that year, escaped the fire. This view shows trolleys pausing at Hudson Place, looking south at the smoldering remains. (William B. Barry photograph, DL&W Collection, Syracuse University.)

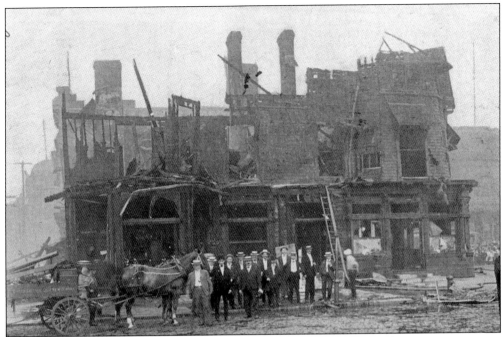

This view looking west shows the extensive fire damage to Duke's House. A temporary structure was soon constructed as an enclosure for ferry offices. The fire damage was the subject of many postcard views, which capitalized upon the disaster while celebrating the rebuilding efforts. (Author's collection.)

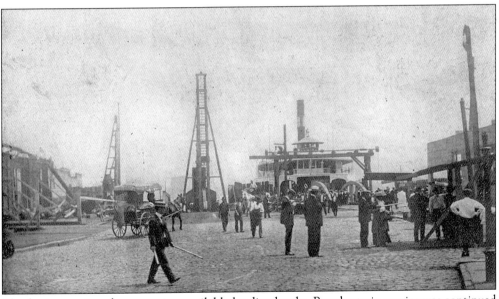

The ferries continued to run using available landing berths. Regular train service was continued with a temporary station installed at the United States Express Building, 100 feet west of the former passenger station. By the afternoon of the day following the fire, two ferry slips were functioning, with boats alternating between the Newark and 14th Street stations in Hoboken. (Author's collection.)

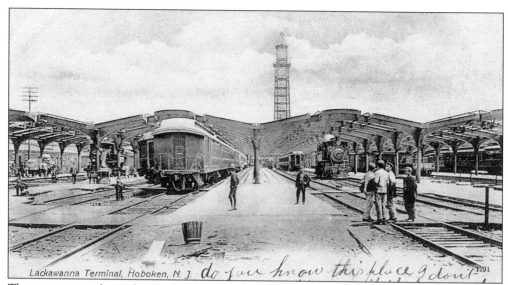

Lackawanna Terminal, Hoboken, N. J. *do you know this place? I don't* 1291

The new terminal was designed to be entirely fireproof and featured many innovations. One of the innovations was the first-ever usage of the design for train sheds developed by the DL&W Chief Engineer Lincoln Bush. The Bush Train Shed replaced the conventional high, arched-roofed train sheds with a system that provided ventilation above the engines, while providing light penetration. (Author's collection.)

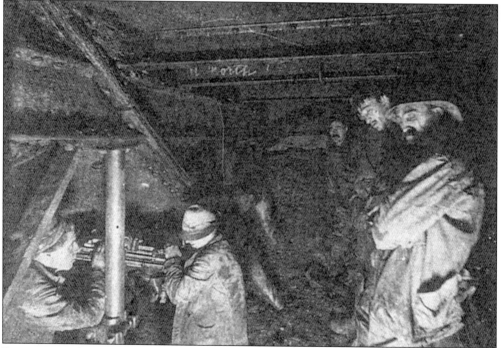

Progress was also being made on the Hudson and Manhattan Rapid Transit (PATH service) with the tunnels being dug to link commuters with trolley, rail, and ferry connections. In this unique photograph, taken in 1902, the worker to the right closes his eyes, perhaps in a moment of prayer, as other men prepare to shove the airtight shield forward. (Courtesy PATH, Trans-Hudson Corporation Archives.)

18

Two

THE GREAT TERMINAL

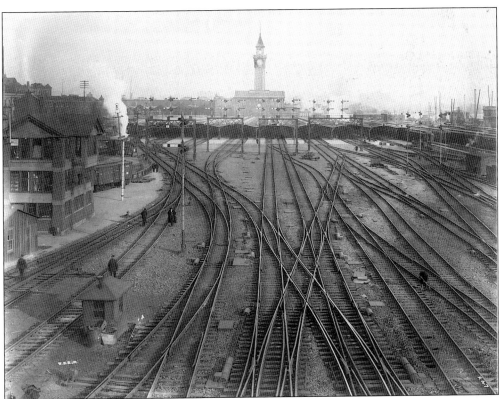

This remarkable c. 1910 bird's-eye view, looking east toward the clock tower of the DL&W Rail and Ferry Terminal, was taken by William B. Barry. This chapter will examine aspects of the terminal complex that have historically distinguished it through design innovation. The new, copper-clad terminal, designed by architect Kenneth M. Murchison, opened at 6 a.m. on February 25, 1907. (DL&W Collection, Syracuse University.)

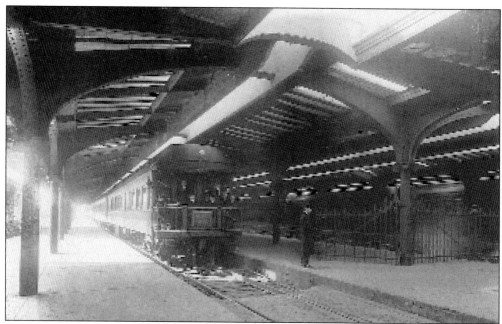

The flagship *Lackawanna Limited* is about to depart Track 15 at Hoboken Terminal as passengers remain on the observation car's open platform. The train ran to Buffalo, and featured a through sleeping car over the Nickel Plate to Chicago. It was replaced by the *Phoebe Snow* in 1949. (William B. Barry, photographer, DL&W Collection, Syracuse University.)

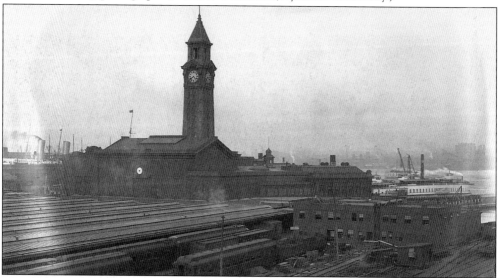

The colossal clock tower, which featured a clock face for each side, rose to a height of 225 feet above the terminal. In this view, taken by William B. Barry from the roof of the powerhouse to the south, the Immigration and Baggage Buildings can be seen to the right. The DL&W had constructed those buildings in July of 1905, the month before the fire, in anticipation of the eventual replacement of the entire complex. Immigrants who had been processed at Ellis Island, who arrived from third class or steerage of transatlantic ships, were given a segregated waiting room from which to board trains to the west and north. (DL&W Collection, Syracuse University.)

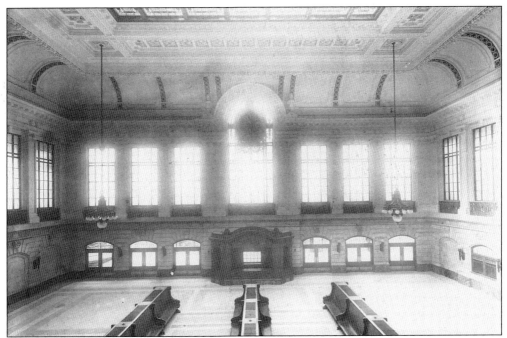

The main waiting room of the terminal is perhaps its most impressive interior space. This view, taken from the upper stairway looking out over the nearly completed room, shows the benches in place. The geometric patterning of the gray and green terrazzo flooring is particularly evident through light, diffused by the multi-paned, opaque high windows. (Courtesy New Jersey Transit.)

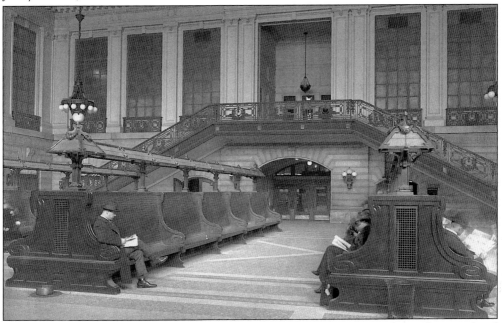

This view, looking toward the stair leading toward the ferry concourses, shows the completed waiting room as it appeared in 1917, with built-in banks of art-glass lighting over the contoured wooden benches. (DL&W Collection, Syracuse University.)

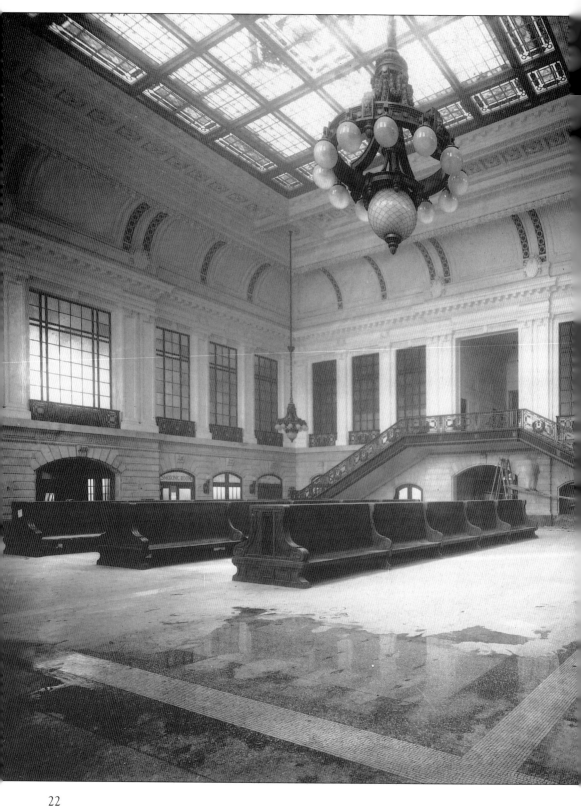

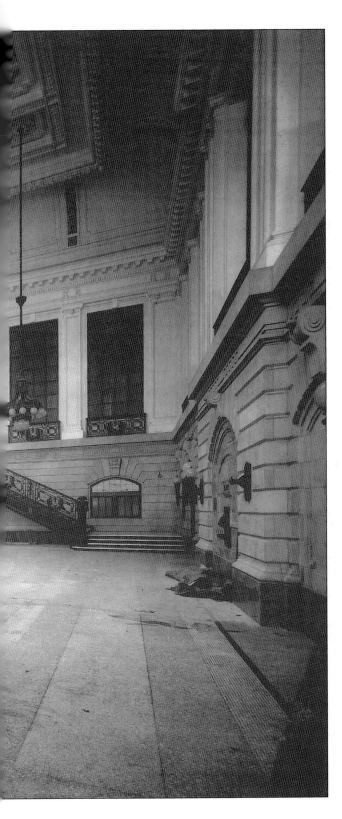

The main waiting room measures 90 by 100 feet and is 55 feet high. Set within the coved ceiling is an impressive art-glass skylight that transmitted natural light by day and was backlit by 1,000 incandescent lights at night. The bronze chandeliers, suspended from the corners, each weighed one ton. (DL&W Collection, Syracuse University.)

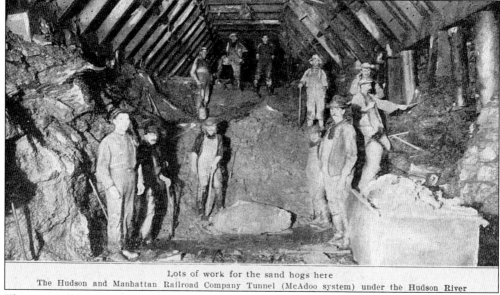

Lots of work for the sand hogs here
The Hudson and Manhattan Railroad Company Tunnel (McAdoo system) under the Hudson River

This view of the "sand hogs" at work was reprinted as a postcard in 1908, from the *Hudson and Manhattan Tunnels*, by The American Photograph Company of New York. (Author's collection.)

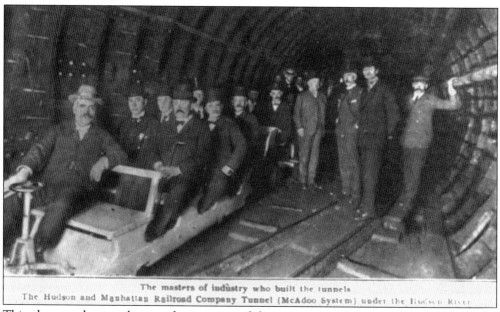

The masters of industry who built the tunnels
The Hudson and Manhattan Railroad Company Tunnel (McAdoo System) under the Hudson River

This photograph was taken on the occasion of the inspection of the completed work on the Hudson and Manhattan tunnels. The man to the right is financier and company president William McAdoo. (Author's collection.)

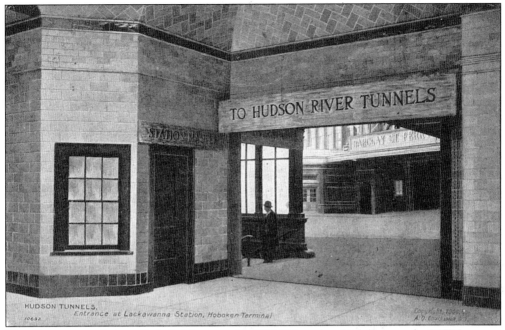

This Guastavino-tiled vestibule led down to the H&M Tunnels, which became the PATH system. In the background is the ramp leading to the Barclay Street ferry entrance. (Author's collection.)

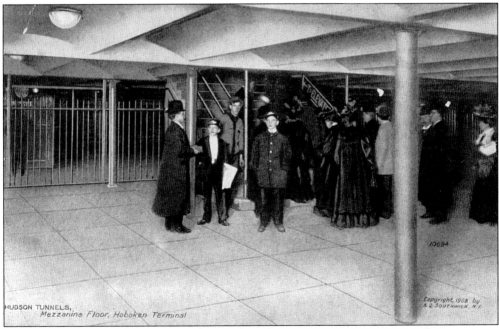

The completion of the H&M Tunnels must have been an exciting innovation for commuters of the day. This postcard, sent in July of 1908 to an Ohio address from Hoboken, stated the following: "Just came from New York to Hoboken, New Jersey in the tunnel under the river over a mile long." (Author's collection.)

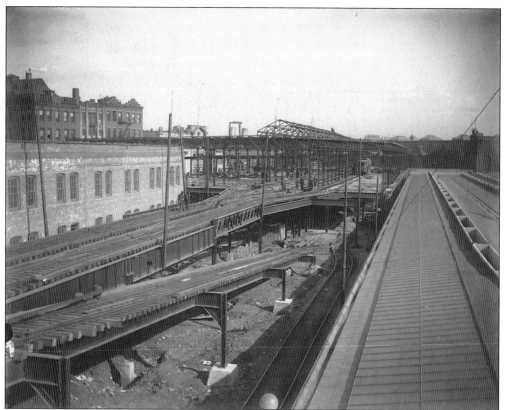

This view, looking east toward the Hoboken Terminal, shows the Public Service Terminal under construction in February of 1910. The skylights and lateral steam vents of the northernmost Bush Train Sheds are visible to the right. (Ira Deutsch Collection, North Jersey Electric Railway Historical Society.)

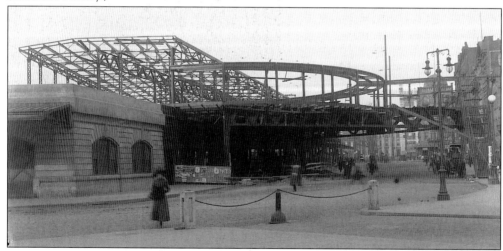

The rounded second-story steel-frame cantilevered trough of the Public Service Trolley Terminal extended over Hudson Place in this February 1910 photograph. A pedestrian walkway extended to the sidewalk in front of the Duke's House site. (Ira Deutsch Collection, North Jersey Electric Railway Historical Society.)

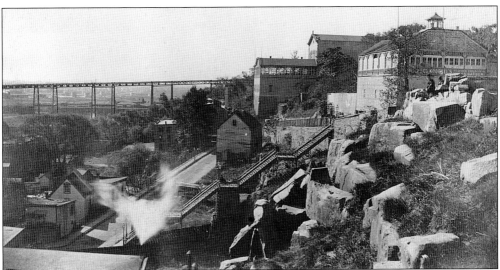

Construction of the Hoboken Inclined Cable Railway was begun in 1882. Completed in 1885, it augmented service on the North Hudson Railway Company's horse car elevator. Considered at one time to be the largest wrought-iron structure in the world, it spanned Jersey City Heights and Hoboken Terminal. This photograph, taken from a perch high above Hoboken, shows the tallest portion, which rose 95 feet above the meadows. In the 1940s, bus service replaced "the elevated." (Willenborg Family Collection, courtesy of *Hoboken Almanac*, copyright Benedict J. Fernandez.)

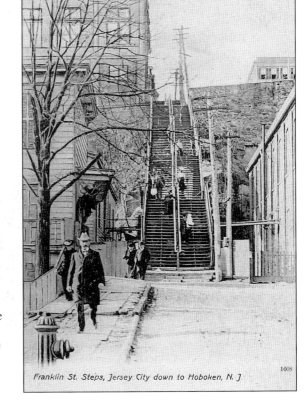

This postcard shows a front view of the stairway to the right in the above photograph. The "Franklin Street Steps" connected Hoboken with Jersey City Heights. The nearest horse car or trolley link was on Willow Street. The steps were designed in the 1880s, by architect/engineer Albert Beyer, who was a Hoboken resident. (Author's collection.)

Franklin St. Steps, Jersey City down to Hoboken, N. J.

1608

27

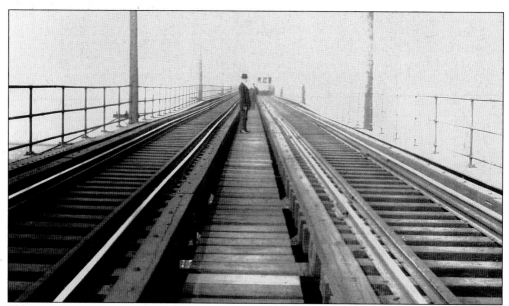

This view, taken from the Hoboken Elevated Railway looking west, shows the steep incline toward the line's highest point. In this October 1915 view, a trolley is proceeding up the westward track, which had been electrified by 1892. The guardrails were riveted to iron plates that supported 67-pound steel rails, laid on white oak beams. (Ira Deutsch Collection, North Jersey Electric Railway Historical Society.)

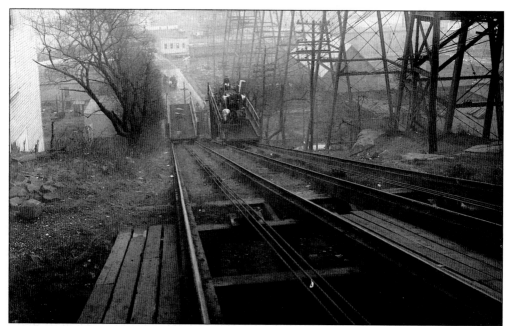

After 1885, the horse car elevator continued to be used for wagons and pedestrians. In this January 1915 view, looking east to Hoboken from the summit, the wagon lift to the right is carrying two loaded wagons, three people, and two horses while two wagons wait at the base. The ride took one minute, but the waiting time could be considerable. (Ira Deutsch Collection, North Jersey Electric Railway Historical Society.)

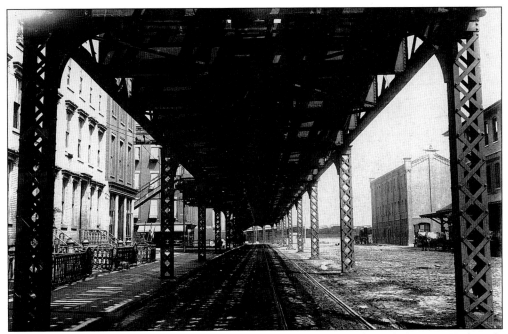

This view, looking toward the Hoboken Terminal down Ferry Street (Observer Highway), shows the underside of the elevated trolley line with its open girders in July of 1911. The 1901 Records Building is to the right. (Ira Deutsch Collection, North Jersey Electric Railway Historical Society.)

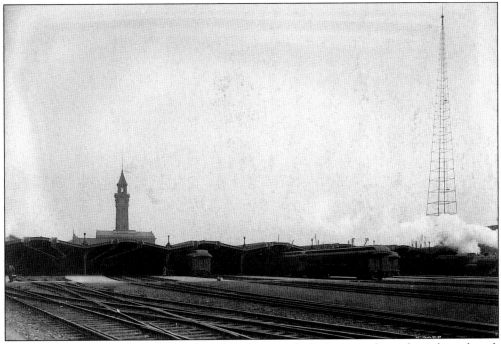

The wireless tower, to the right, in this 1910 photograph, looking southeast from the rail yard, was used in communication between the terminal and arriving trains. (DL&W Collection, Syracuse University.)

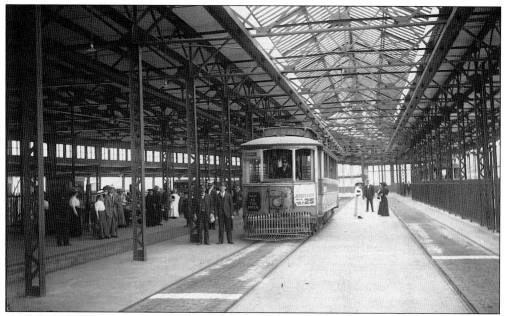

A Union Hill trolley arrives at the Public Service Trolley Terminal in this interior view, showing the extensive skylight system. The cars of the elevated proceeded into the terminal solely on momentum, making for an especially thrilling ride under icy conditions. Cars entered and exited the terminal under one switch. (Ira Deutsch Collection, North Jersey Electric Railway Historical Society.)

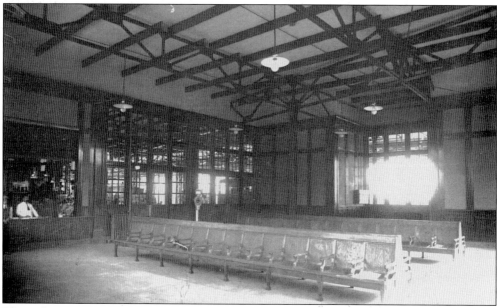

The utilitarian waiting room of the Public Service Trolley Terminal featured wooden benches with armrests and ample windows to see the approach of cars from the adjoining platform level. (Ira Deutsch Collection, North Jersey Electric Railway Historical Society.)

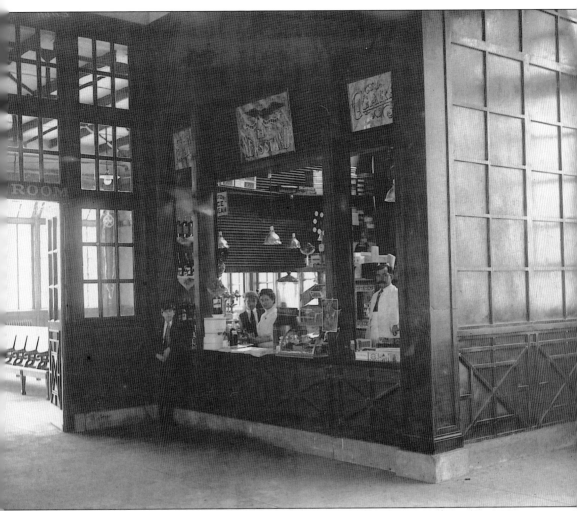

The newsstand of the Public Service Trolley Terminal adjoined the waiting room area. This intriguing photograph, taken at five minutes to three on a July afternoon in 1910, reveals that cigars, grape soda, and orangeade were among the offerings available to commuters. (Ira Deutsch Collection, North Jersey Electric Railway Historical Society.)

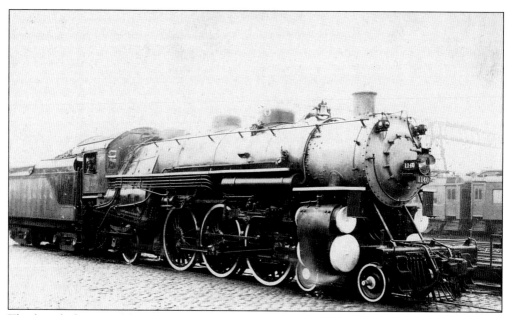

This broadside view of the Pacific-type engine, Number 1140, shows that it is of a "4-6-2" wheel configuration. (Author's collection.)

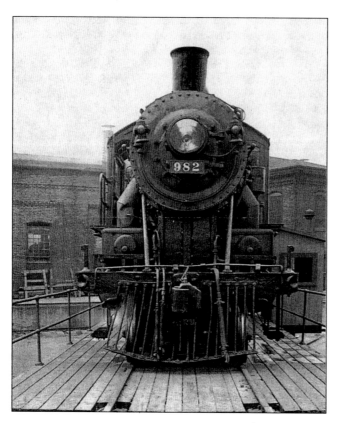

In this William B. Barry photograph, engine Number 982 is positioned on a Lassig turntable outside the brick roundhouse that was once at the Hoboken yard. Turntables enabled the steam engines to be reversed. (John Willever Collection, courtesy Beyer, Blinder, Belle.)

This impressive bronze statue at the terminus of Hudson Place honors Sam Sloan, who served as a director of the DL&W in 1864, as president from 1867 to 1899, and chairman until his death in 1907. During Sloan's administration, no trains were run on Sundays. The statue was originally placed facing outward toward the ferry plaza on the once cobblestone area. It now faces toward the city of Hoboken and is set within a repaved, landscaped plaza with the ferry slips as its backdrop. Both the bronze statue and the copper of the terminal façade have attained the same distinctive green patina. (Author's collection.)

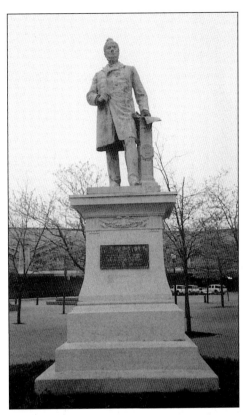

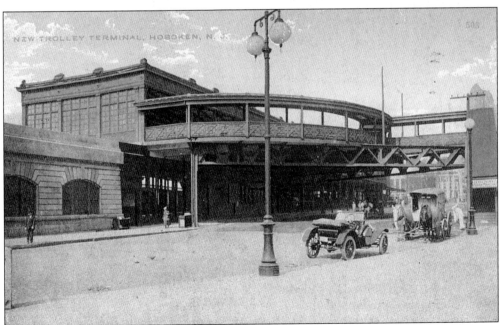

The completed Public Service Trolley Terminal, is seen from Hudson Place looking southwest, c. 1913, before the YMCA added additional stories onto the baggage area of the rail terminal. (Author's collection.)

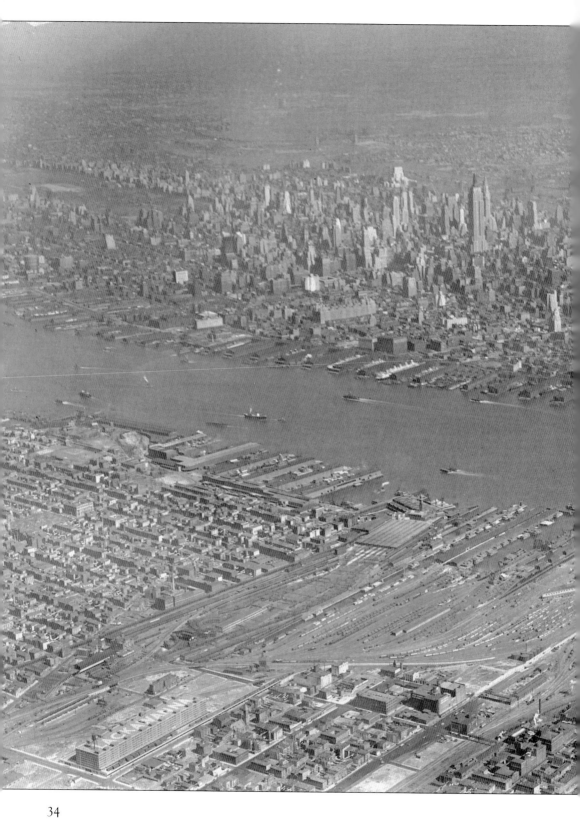

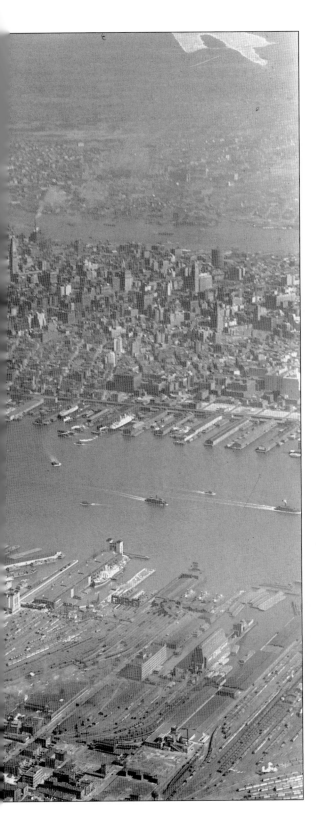

This Dallin aerial photograph overlooking the eastern portion of the city of Hoboken, and beyond, was taken on March 19, 1931. One of the striking elements of this view is the network of intersecting rail lines, which surround Hoboken and Jersey City, forming vital commercial links. The advent of electrified service on the Lackawanna Railroad was inaugurated by Thomas A. Edison on September 3, 1930, who operated a train for a short distance out of Hoboken Terminal. On September 22 of the same year, Edison started the first electric train through the Oranges in another event which drew considerable publicity. (Hagley Museum and Library.)

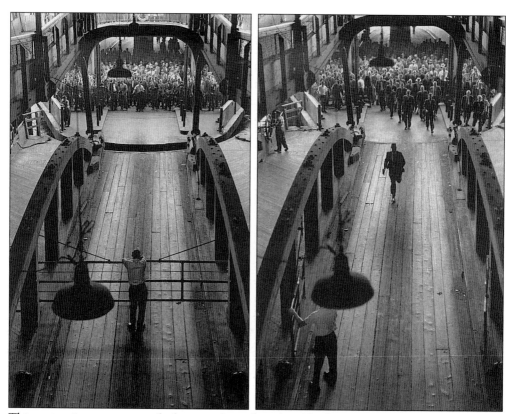

This evocative sequence of photographs, taken by Charles Pratt in 1966, captures the choreography of an evening's commute, with ferry passengers arriving from Manhattan as they

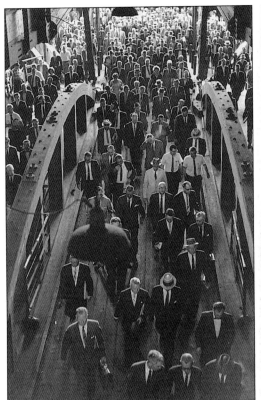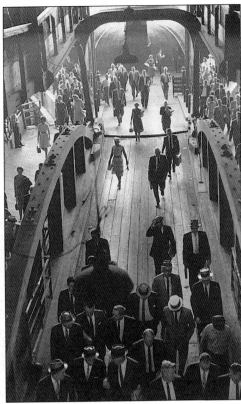

sprint across the Stern patent bridge that adjusted with the shifting level of the tide. One can almost smell the brackish water and creosote of the pilings. (Courtesy Mrs. Julia Pratt.)

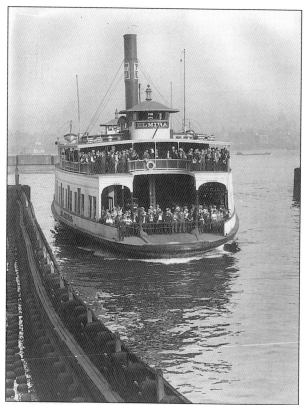

The *Elmira*, together with the *Binghamton* and *Scandinavia*, represented advancements in speed and safety. They were built in 1905 by the Newport News Ship Building and Dry Dock Company of Virginia for the Lackawanna Railroad. (Courtesy Keystone-Mast Collection UCR/California Museum of Photography, University of California, Riverside. Neg. #KU86178.)

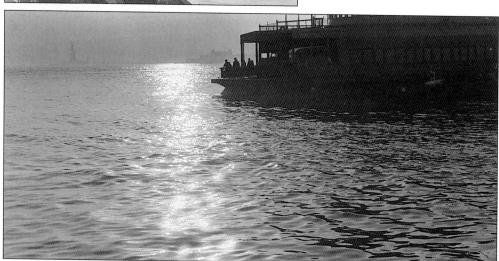

This photograph by Charles Pratt was taken shortly before ferry service was discontinued in 1967. This and other of the photographer's work was featured in the Regional Plan Association's landmark study *The Lower Hudson* in 1966. The Statue of Liberty is visible to the left while a ferryboat is silhouetted by the late afternoon sun. Writing of his memories of commuting via ferry in the 1930s, in his book *American Ferryboats*, John Perry recalled: ". . . this voyage was a peaceful bridge between work and home. We stood on the upper deck, heads bared to the evening breeze, watching the lights come on, leaving the city . . . For dreamers it was the stuff of a million dreams . . . ." (Courtesy Mrs. Julie Pratt.)

Three

CENTER OF COMMERCE

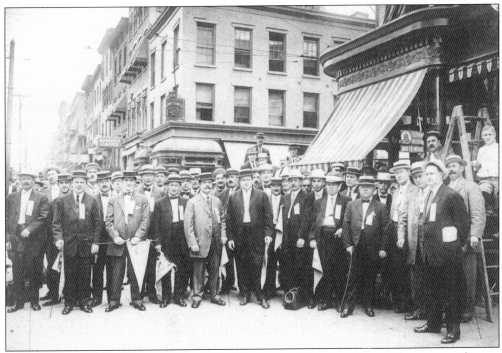

The area surrounding the terminal and the lower waterfront experienced the greatest changes over time, when the area expanded out over the river. With transportation becoming more available, the terminal area became a transportation hub, as well as a center of commerce. By the late 1890s, Hoboken's terminal area and downtown were graced with many impressive bank and office buildings. In this photograph, dated June 26, 1912, delegates to the Democratic Convention gathered on Washington Street in front of the southeast corner of Newark Street. (Courtesy Hoboken Public Library.)

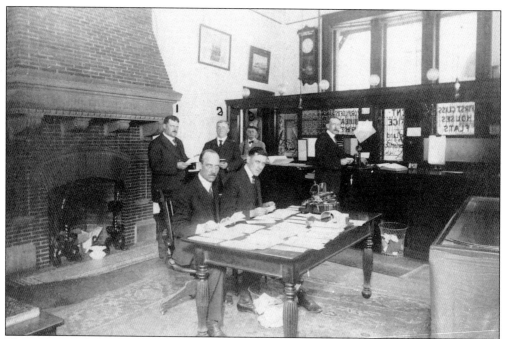

This photograph gives a view of one of the offices at the Hoboken Land and Improvement Building c. 1900. The individuals identified by number on the photograph are #1 Mr. Grouls, #2 Mr. Fitzimmon, and #3 Mr. Eddie Odell (letter carrier number 1). The leaded-glass leading on the work counter reads: "first class hotels and flats." (Courtesy Hoboken Public Library.)

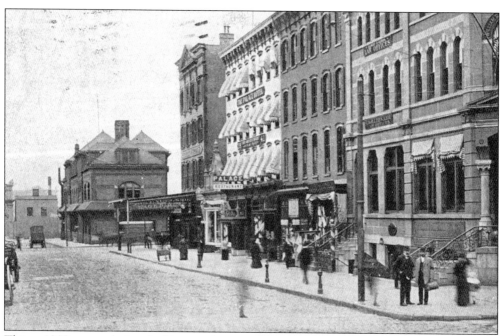

This c. 1908 postcard view, looking southeast on Newark Street, shows the Hoboken Land and Improvement Building, to the left, and the corner bank building. (Author's collection.)

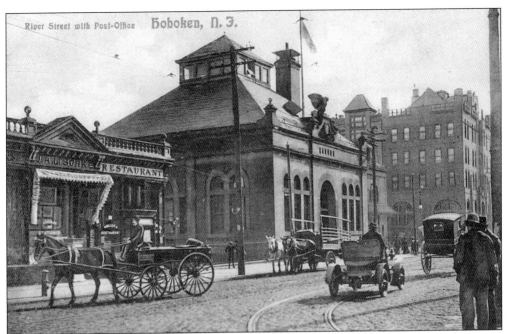

The River Street post office is in the center of this busy streetscape view. To the right, in the postcard, is the Second National Bank Building located on the corner of River Street and Hudson Place. Constructed in 1888, the bank's basement was the first home of the Hoboken Public Library prior to the construction of the permanent library building on Fifth Street in 1897. The bank features "battered" or inclined foundation walls and large, Romanesque arches. (Author's collection.)

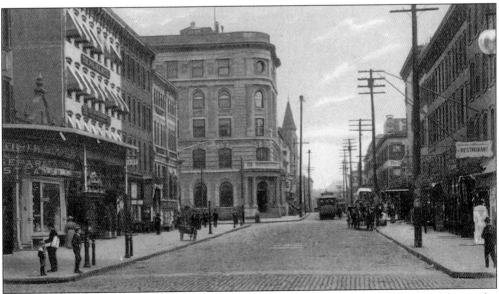

This postcard view is looking westward on Newark Street. The buildings to the right, in the foreground, housed Servanti's Restaurant, which became the famed Clam Broth House. The establishment has had only three owners since it opened in 1899. (Author's collection.)

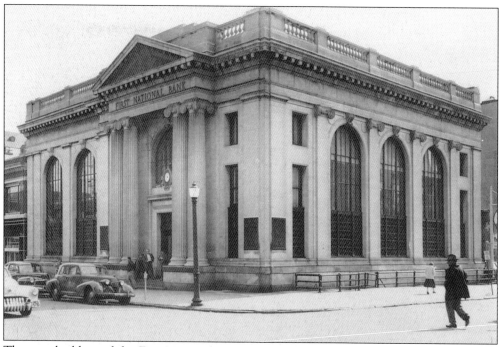

The new building of the First National Bank was designed by Kenneth M. Murchison, who also designed the 1907 Hoboken Terminal. It was constructed of South Dover marble in 1909, at which time it was considered "a simple classic design . . . the most dignified and appropriate style for such an institution." (Courtesy Hoboken Public Library.)

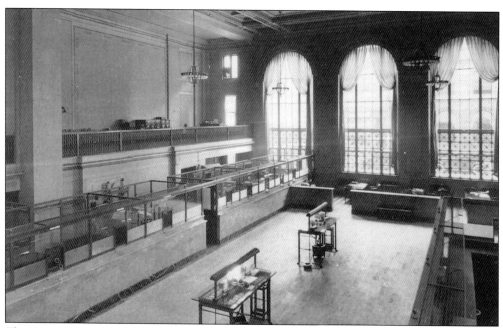

The First National Bank's interior featured all working space contained on one floor, the use of Greek marble on walls and bases, as well as a large skylight above. This photograph dates from the 1950s. (Courtesy Hoboken Public Library.)

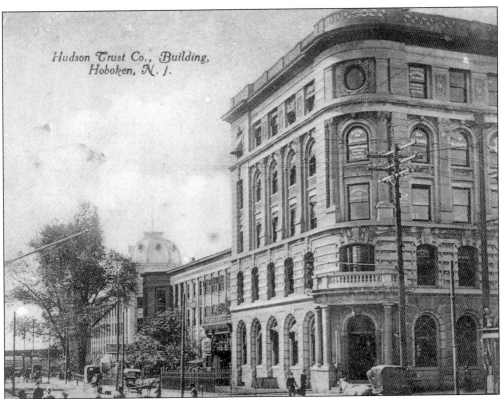

This postcard view looking south on Hudson Street, with the Hudson Trust Company in the foreground, shows the buildings dating from the 1850s to the south of the bank. The three-story brick rowhouses featured pilasters resembling a colonnade, which extended around the entire block. The domed building was the Eagan Business School. (Courtesy Hoboken Public Library.)

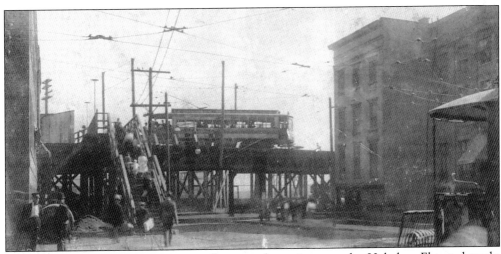

This photograph shows commuters walking up the stairway to the Hoboken Elevated tracks at Ferry Street, at the corner of Hudson Street. In the foreground, to the right, is a glimpse through the front of a trolley, with the conductor's lever and formidable "people catcher," a safety feature, extending from the front of the car. (Courtesy Hoboken Public Library.)

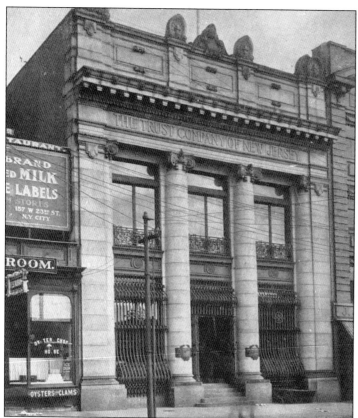

Another of the Neoclassical, colossally scaled bank buildings of the downtown area was the Trust Company of New Jersey's building, on Hudson Place, seen here in a published photograph in 1909. Its two-story-high, marble columns with Ionic capitals complement the style of the Hoboken Terminal. Like the 1887 Hoboken Evening News building, also on the same block, the Trust Company has an identical façade on the north side that faces the private cobblestone cartway at the foot of Newark Street, alongside the Land and Improvement Building. (Hoboken Public Library.)

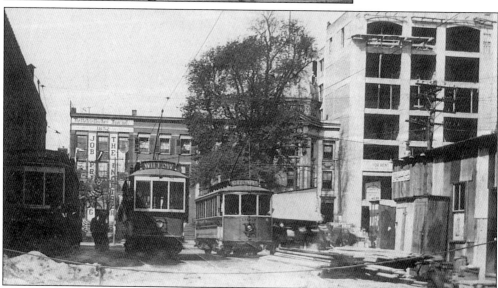

The Willow, Grove, and Washington Street trolley lines of the Hudson Division terminated at Hudson Place. In this view, much construction is underway. This photograph predates the construction of the Hotel Victor, at the southeast corner of Hudson Street and Hudson Place. Also, the Terminal Office Building was under construction c. 1910. (Collection of A.W. Mankoff.)

The Terminal Office Building features an unusual use of Art Nouveau ornamentation on its façade, which is seven stories high and faces the river. At each end of the parapet is a large head of the Egyptian goddess Hathor, goddess of the sky. Strikingly similar motifs were used at the 1902 Exhibition of Modern Decorative Art's Belgian Gallery, designed by the Austrian-educated architect, Raimondo D'Aronco. The name of the building appears on a plaque set into the parapet, flanked by representations of the menat, the ancient Egyptian sun-symbol. The lobby still retains its original decorative elements. (Postcard from the author's collection.)

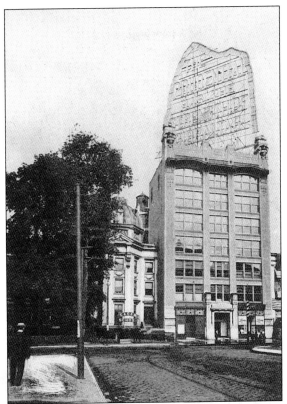

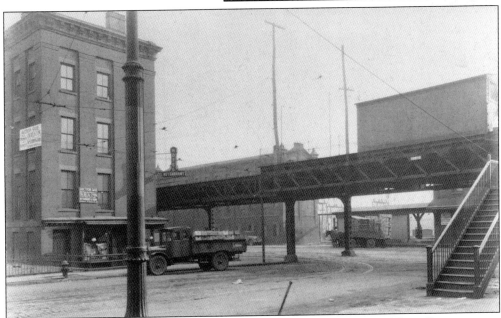

In this photograph by William B. Barry, at the intersection of Hudson and Ferry Streets, we see that the building to the left is to be subject to an auction sale. A fruit truck is parked in front, while horse-drawn carts pause along Ferry Street. This building may have been purchased in the Public Service expansion of the terminal facilities. (DL&W Collection, Syracuse University.)

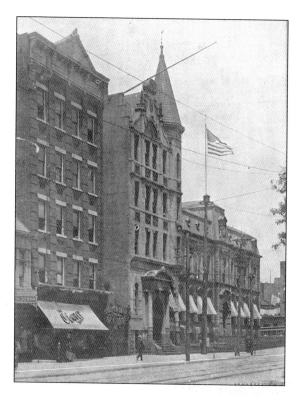

The turreted Hoboken Bank for Savings, at the corner of Washington and Newark Streets, is seen in this *c.* 1906 postcard view published by E.F. Walter that looks north along Washington Street. The bank, founded in 1857, occupies a brick and brownstone Northern Renaissance Revival–style building that is the 1890 design of the noted New York architectural firm, Napoleon LeBrun & Sons. It once housed Hoboken's first telephone exchange. (Courtesy Hoboken Public Library.)

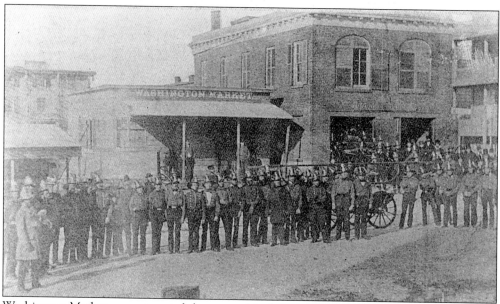

Washington Market once occupied the square block that is now the location of city hall. This undated photograph shows members of the Washington Hook & Ladder Company and, to the right, Hoboken Engine Company Number 1. At that time, "Town Hall" was over the Engine House (to the right). In preparation for the construction of city hall, buildings were removed and even squatters relocated. (Willenborg Family Collection, courtesy *Hoboken Almanac*, copyright Benedict J. Fernandez.)

The European-born Hoboken resident Francis George Himpler was the architect of Hoboken's City Hall. Among his designs are Saints Peter and Paul in St. Louis, Missouri, St. Mary's (Our Lady of Grace), Academy of the Sacred Heart in Hoboken, as well as private residences. (1893 photograph from *The Evening News & Hoboken*.)

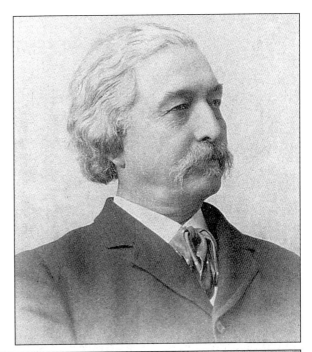

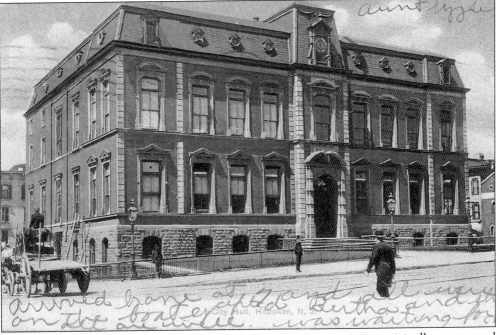

Hoboken's City Hall had a distinct Second Empire appearance as it was originally constructed in 1883. The building combined red brick with brownstone trimming the windows, doors, and rustic basement. The grassy area on either side of the entry was intended for plantings. In this postcard view, a wagon is headed west on Newark Street. The building was enlarged in 1912–1913 by architects Schnieder and Dieffenback. Their design added space and a monumental stairway, but caused the removal of the earlier brownstone trim, to the dismay of the original architect. (Author's collection.)

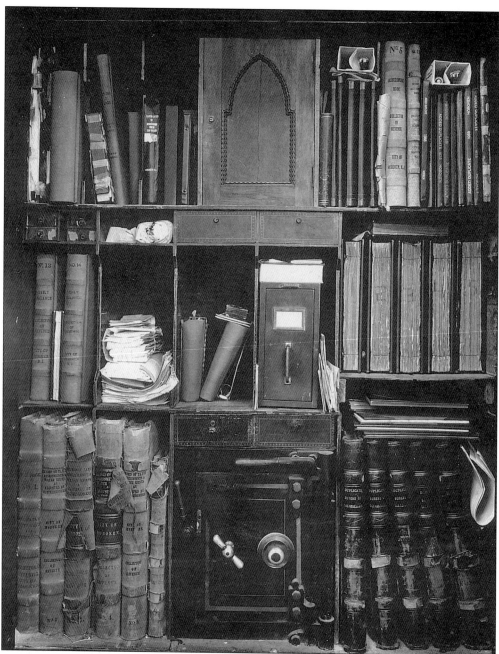

Hoboken's City Hall once had two formidable vaults with colorful, hand-painted doors in its offices. The interior of the one above (left) bore colorful painted panels of the city mascot, the state seal, and the city hall building, with horse cars in the street. It was originally in the Collector of Revenue's office. The other features an early baseball game between the "Jersey Jays" and the New York Fire Department, presumably in Hoboken's Elysian Fields. The panels

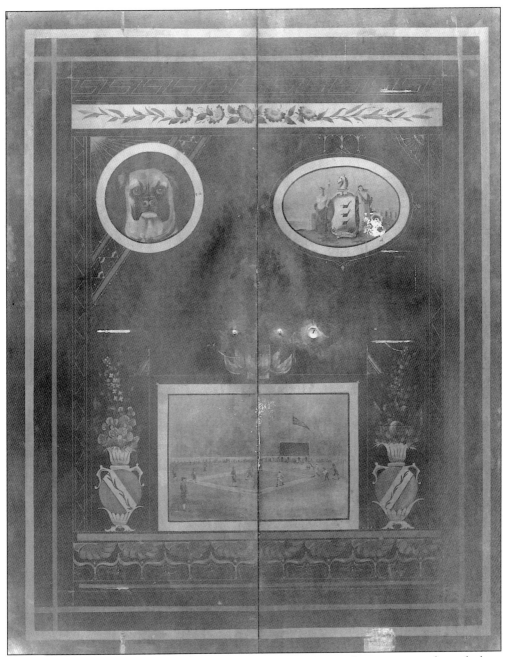

measure 52 inches wide by over 63 inches high and were painted on quarter-inch steel plate, each set weighing 300 pounds. Although the vaults have since been discarded, the City has retained the panels. Photographer Steve Zane recorded the vault interior and painted panels in 1981, shortly before their removal. City hall, a *National Register* site, was included in the book *America's City Halls* in 1984. (Courtesy Steve Zane.)

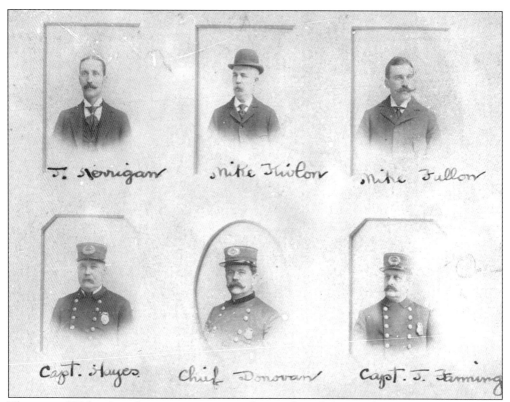

These pre-1915 police department portraits depict, from left to right, as follows: (bottom) Captain Hayes, Chief Donovan, and Captain J. Fanning; (top) J. Kerrigan, Mike Kivlon, and Mike Fallon. A paid police force was established in 1891. (Courtesy Hoboken Public Library.)

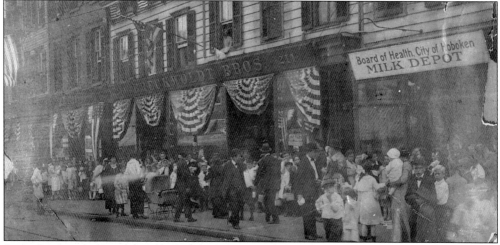

In the Progressive Era, city government sought to improve the nutrition of the local children by distributing milk through its Department of Health at this "milk depot," set up in a storefront at 209–211 First Street. Note that parents and children are holding metal containers to be filled. The milk supply arrived in glass-lined tank train cars, cooled by ice blocks, via the railroad's milk depot in the Railway Express Building on Ferry Street. (Courtesy Hoboken Public Library.)

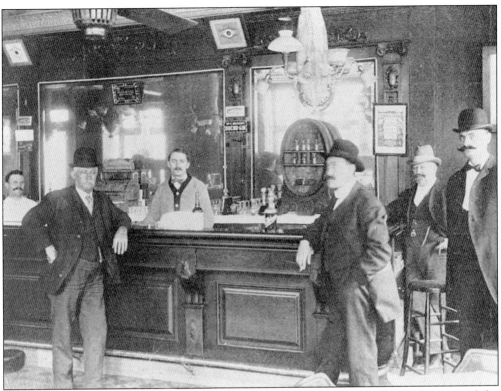

Captain Emil Berckmann, pictured in this 1909 photograph, was a noted sharpshooter and the proprietor of a popular bar and café at 200 Bloomfield Street. (Willenborg Family Collection, courtesy *Hoboken Almanac*, copyright Benedict J. Fernandez.)

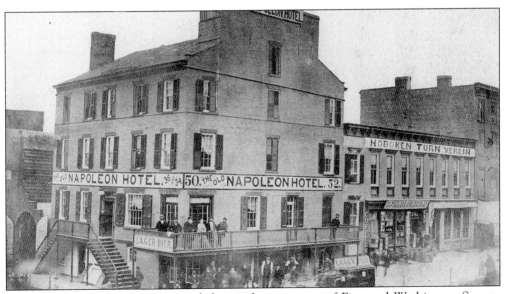

The Napoleon Hotel once occupied the northwest corner of First and Washington Streets. The *Turn Verein*, or German gymnasium, was located to the north in this *c.* 1871 photograph. (Courtesy Hoboken Public Library.)

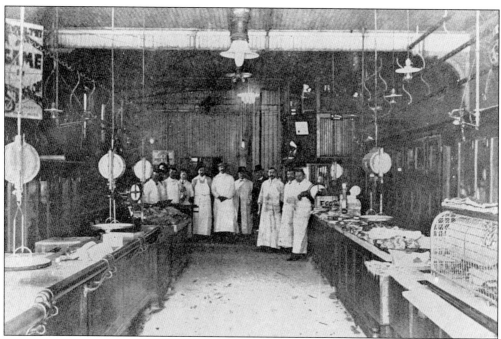

This *c.* 1909 view shows the Washington Street meat market of M. Strohmeier & Brothers. (Willenborg Family Collection, courtesy *Hoboken Almanac*, copyright Benedict J. Fernandez.)

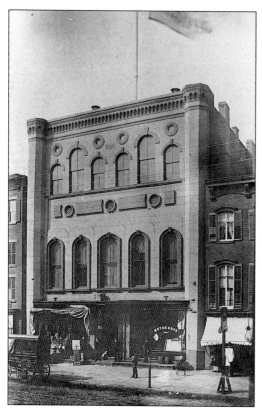

The Odd Fellows Hall (completed by 1854), at Washington Street, was the location of many social gatherings, meetings, as well as the temporary location of worship services for religious congregations prior to the construction of permanent buildings. (Willenborg Family Collection, courtesy *Hoboken Almanac*, copyright Benedict J. Fernandez.)

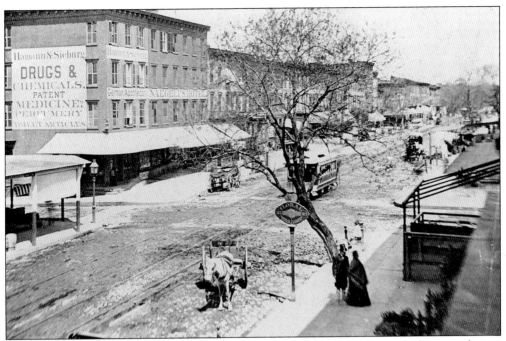

This photograph, taken from an upper window along Washington Street looking northwest, shows horse cars and carts in the street. Naegeli's Hotel occupied the building just north of the Fourth Street corner. Note the many awnings projecting from the buildings. (Willenborg Family Collection, courtesy *Hoboken Almanac*, copyright Benedict J. Fernandez.)

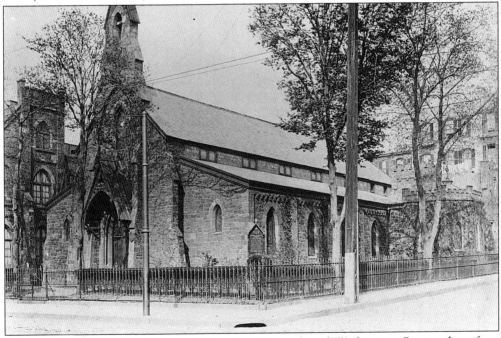

The Gothic-styled Trinity Episcopal Church, at Seventh and Washington Streets, dates from 1856 with an addition in 1882. (Willenborg Family Collection, courtesy *Hoboken Almanac*, copyright Benedict J. Fernandez.)

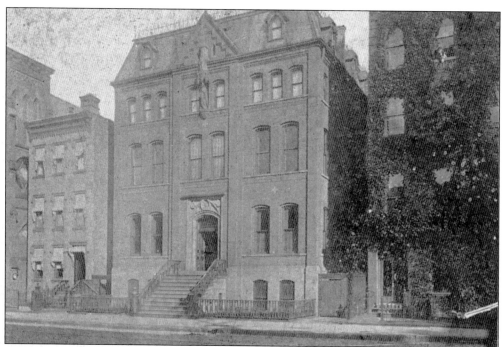

Academy of the Sacred Heart, north of Trinity Episcopal Church, was founded in 1868 by the Sisters of Charity. The mansard-roofed building was designed by Francis George Himpler. (Author's collection.)

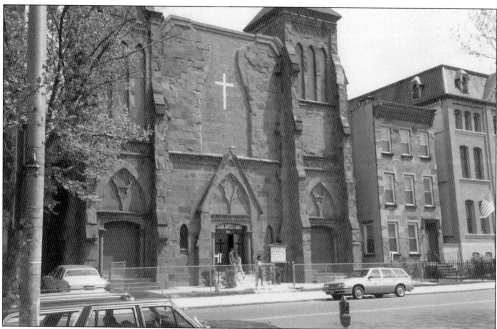

The Mount Olive Baptist Church, founded in 1918, has occupied the former 1871 Methodist Church, a Gothic-styled brownstone church, since 1967. Although a fire severely damaged the interior in 1977, the congregation rebuilt their church around the outer masonry shell. (Author's collection.)

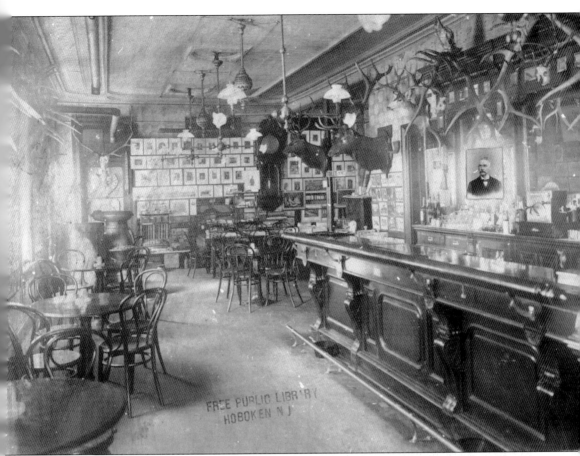

Kaegebehn's was a restaurant frequented by the Elysian Camera Club, as evidenced by the many photographs lining the walls. A publication honoring the work of Hoboken artist Charles Schreyvogel was published by Charles Kaegebehn in 1908. The restaurant was located at 802 Washington Street at that time. (Courtesy Hoboken Public Library.)

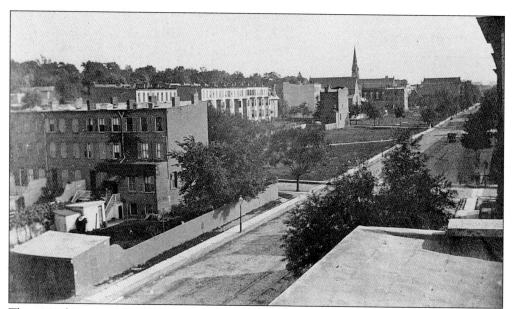

This view from the mid-1880s, taken from a rooftop and looking south on Washington Street at Tenth Street, shows the undeveloped tracts of land that existed at that time. (Willenborg Family Collection, courtesy *Hoboken Almanac*, copyright Benedict J. Fernandez.)

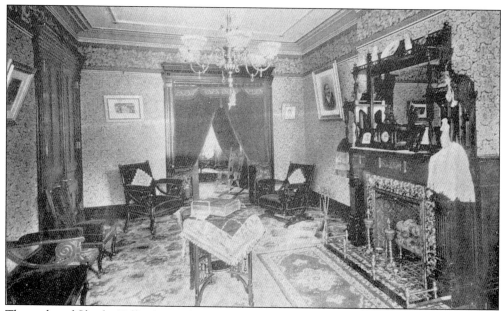

The parlor of Charles Fall's elegant home, at 915 Washington Street, was featured in a write-up about the architect. (*The Evening News & Hoboken*, 1893.)

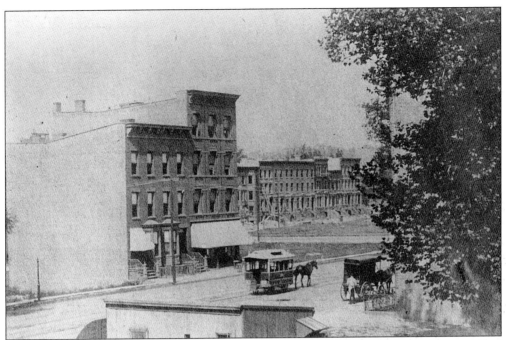

Another view from the same time period, looking northwest from Washington Street toward the corner of Eleventh Street, shows an entire block of brick and brownstone rowhouses under construction. One of these rowhouses was F.G. Himpler's house (second from right) on Bloomfield Street. (Willenborg Family Collection, courtesy *Hoboken Almanac*, copyright Benedict J. Fernandez.)

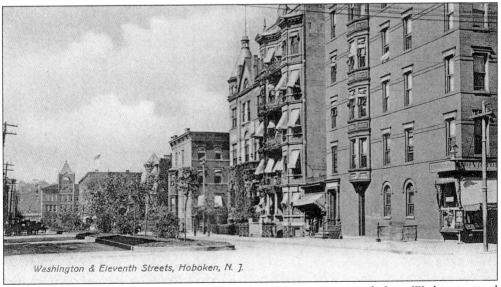

Washington & Eleventh Streets, Hoboken, N. J.

By the 1890s (the date of this postcard), much had been constructed along Washington and Bloomfield Streets. (Author's collection.)

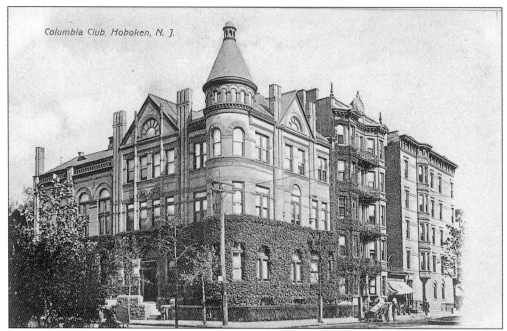

Columbia Club, Hoboken, N. J.

The Richardsonian Romanesque–styled Columbia Club, at the northeast corner of Bloomfield and Eleventh Streets, was built in 1891 as an opulently appointed social club complete with a library, card rooms, and basement bowling alleys. It became the Euclid Masonic Lodge in 1910, followed by several other uses. Its restoration began in 1988, as it was carefully returned to its original elegance. (Author's collection.)

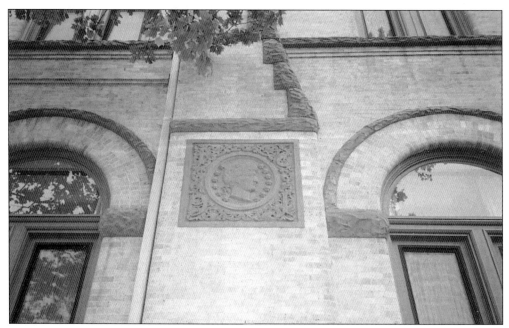

This profile of "Columbia," symbol of progress, graces the Eleventh Street façade of the Columbia Club. It was photographed after the building was restored and layers of paint had been removed from the exterior. (Author's photograph.)

58

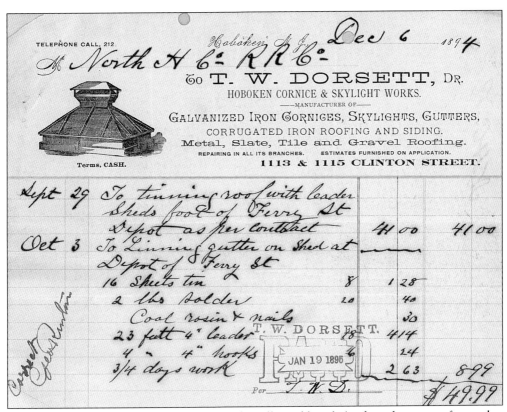

The mass-production of metal cornices, windowsills, and lintels (such as those manufactured at T.W. Dorsett's Hoboken Cornice and Skylight Works, at 1113–1115 Clinton Street) facilitated much of the city's residential construction. (Author's collection.)

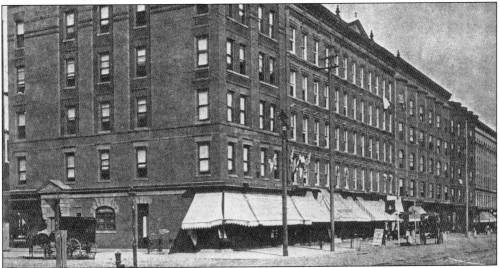

The Eldorado Apartments, beginning at the northwest corner of Twelfth and Washington Streets, were designed in the 1890s by the prolific architect and builder, Hoboken resident Charles Fall. Mr. Fall maintained an office within this building, at 1230 Washington Street. (Author's collection.)

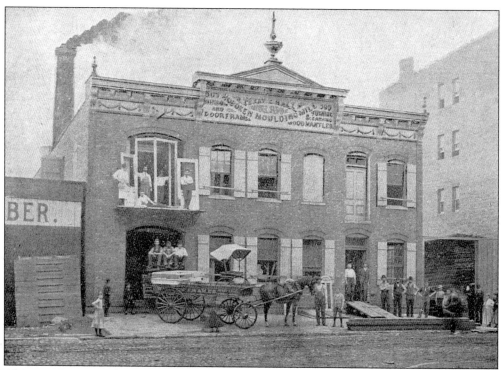

Also contributing to the construction of apartment flats was the Hoboken Moulding Mill, which produced door and window frames as well as wood mantels. (*The Evening News & Hoboken*, 1893.)

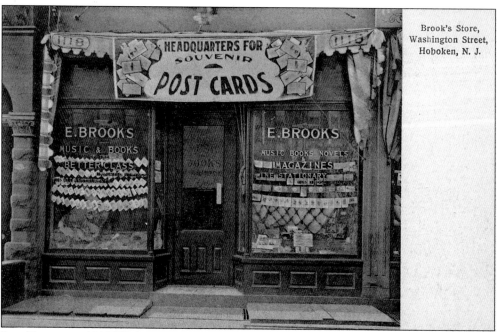

Brook's store, at 1118 Washington Street, sold souvenirs that were self-published and printed in Germany. (Author's collection.)

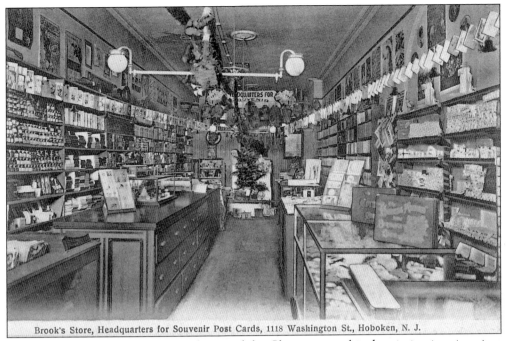

Brook's Store, Headquarters for Souvenir Post Cards, 1118 Washington St., Hoboken, N. J.

The interior of Brook's Store was decorated for Christmas in this descriptive interior view. (Author's collection.)

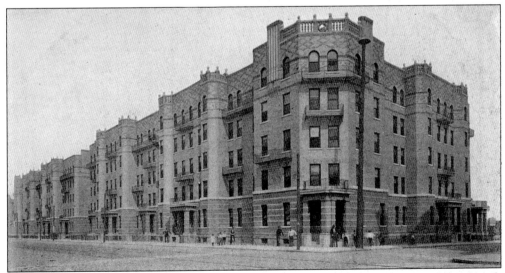

The Elysian Apartments, also known as the "Yellow Flats" because of the yellowish brick with which they were constructed, occupy Washington Street from Twelfth to Thirteenth Streets. The patterned brick of the parapets gives the block a distinctly Jacobean flavor. The legendary millionaire Hetty Green resided here in a cold-water flat. (Author's collection.)

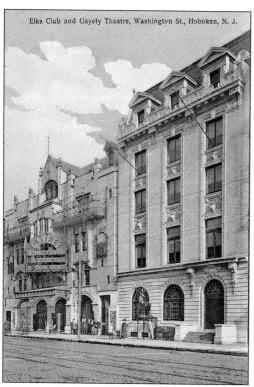

Elks Club and Gayety Theatre, Washington St., Hoboken, N. J.

The Gayety Theatre, formerly the Quartette Club, and the Elks Club made an impressive grouping on the 1200 block of Washington Street. The theatre building was replaced or remodeled by the Washington Arms Apartments. (Author's collection.)

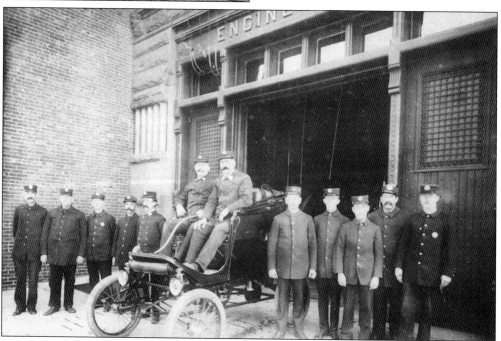

The firehouse at 1313 Washington Street was built in 1890, by the firm French, Dixon & DeSaldern in the Richardsonian Romanesque style. It is set back 12 feet to provide ample distance from tobacco-spitting firemen. The building represents the first time a fire tower was incorporated into the design of a firehouse in Hoboken. (Courtesy Hoboken Public Library.)

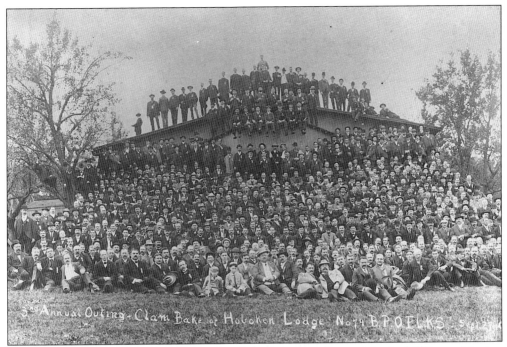

This photograph is a wonderful example of the banquet photographer's skill in positioning his subjects and convincing them to sit still during the long exposure. The photograph, taken by the local postcard publisher K.F. Walter, documents the third annual clambake outing of the Hoboken B.P.O. Elks, on September 27, 1903. (Willenborg Family Collection, courtesy *Hoboken Almanac*, copyright Benedict J. Fernandez.)

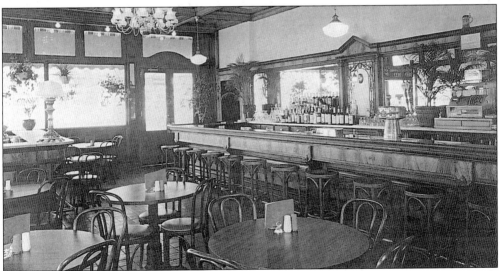

The interior of the American Hotel, at the northwest corner of Washington and Fourteenth Streets, features a lush interior with a burled walnut bar and a beautiful, reverse-painted glass ceiling that was set within wood panels. The storefront was among the first to participate in the Community Development Agency's "Shop" program, which created incentives via low-interest loans for sensitive rehabilitation. (Courtesy Jim Hans.)

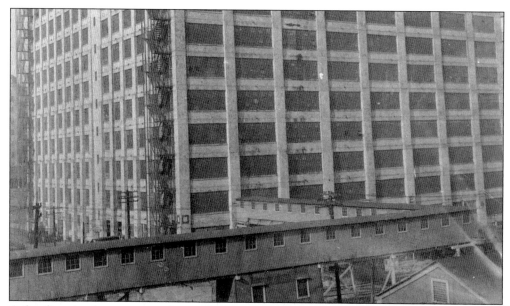

A familiar visual presence at the northern end of Washington Street, the Terminal Building (located on the waterfront at Fifteenth Street) housed the Remington Arms during World War I. Sir Thomas Lipton, the English tea manufacturer and yachtsman, later purchased the building. This photograph dates from 1919. (Courtesy Hoboken Public Library.)

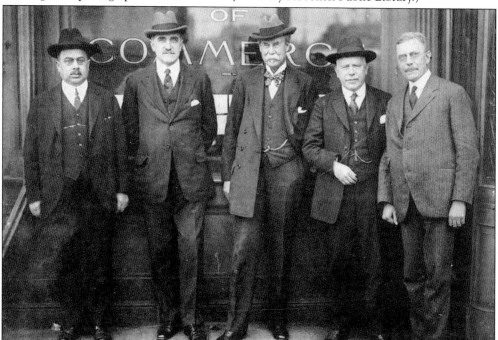

Sir Thomas Lipton became a member of the Hoboken Chamber of Commerce in 1919. The group of businessmen depicted in this image includes the following, from left to right: Max Schalscha, chairman of the Members' Forum, Sir J. Ferguson, Sir Thomas Lipton, C.H.C. Jagels, and Palmer Campbell, Chamber president. (Copyright International Photo, courtesy Hoboken Public Library.)

64

Four

ALONG THE
TROLLEY PATH

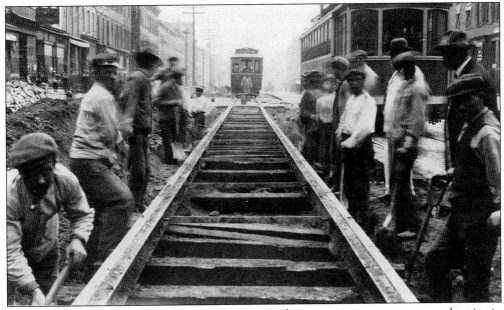

By 1911, Hoboken's Board of Trade was recommending a major improvement to the city in the widening of the distance between trolley tracks on Washington Street and the burying of overhead cables. The Public Service Company began work on Washington Street in 1913. What follows is a unique glimpse into the appearance of Washington Street as documented by a Public Service Company photographer who recorded the progress of the work. This unusual view shows the depth at which the trolley track is laid. This photograph, dating from October 25, 1913, was taken looking north on Washington Street from Sixth Street. (Ira Deutsch Collection, North Jersey Electric Railway Historical Society.)

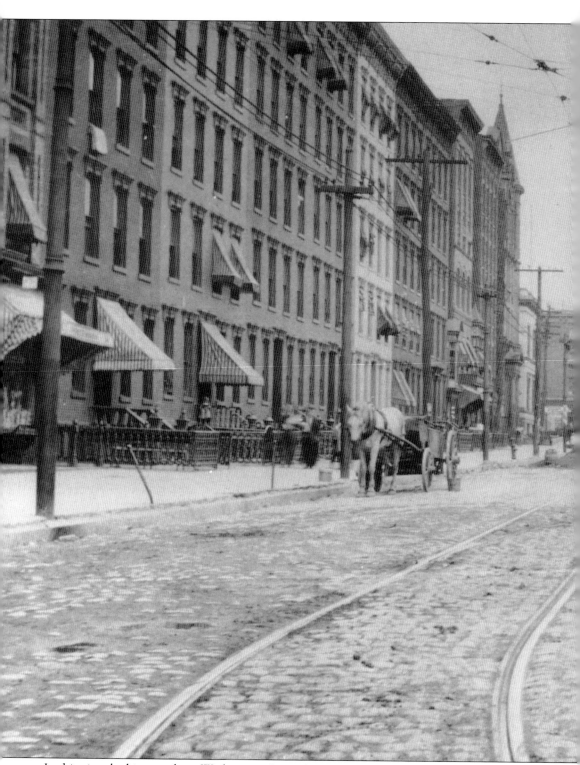

In this view, looking north on Washington Street from Ferry Street on Friday, August 22, 1913, some of the houses that formed Washington Terrace, a block-square housing complex from the

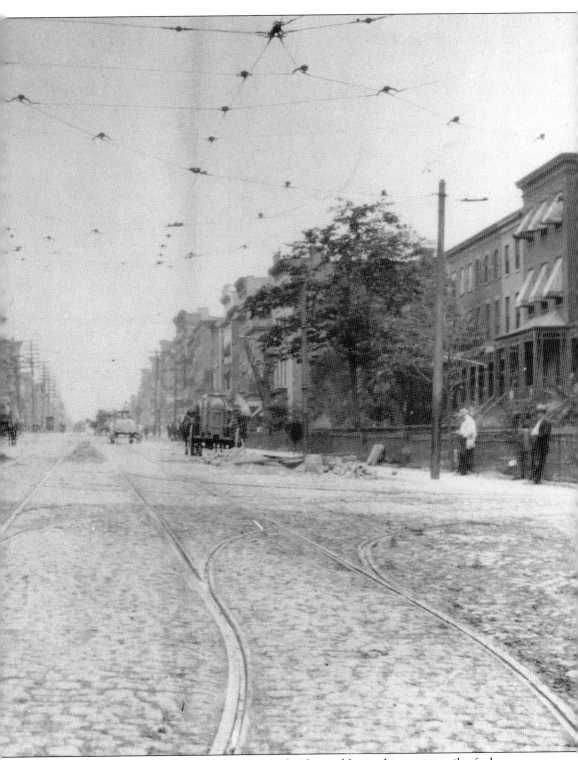

1850s, are visible to the right in the foreground. Also visible are the curving rails of a horse car right-of-way. (Ira Deutsch Collection, North Jersey Electric Railway Historical Society.)

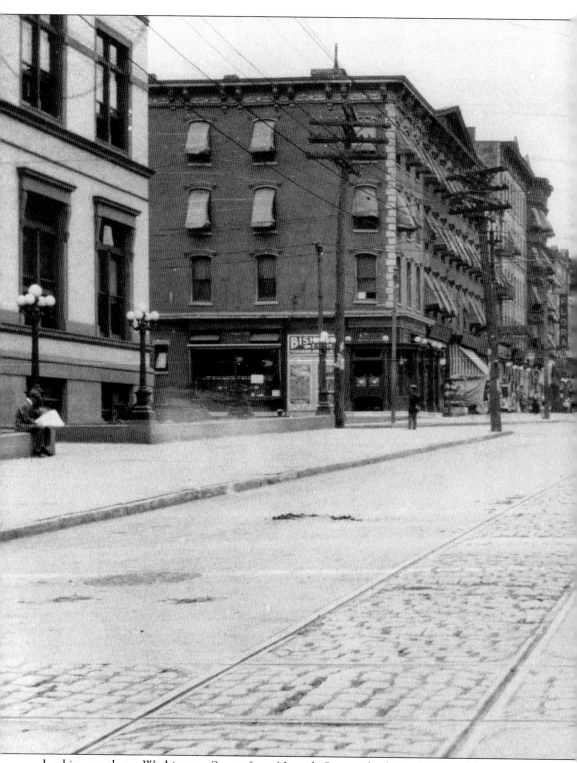

Looking north on Washington Street from Newark Street, the beige brick and brownstone corner of city hall is visible to the left in the foreground. Beyond city hall, on the left, is the

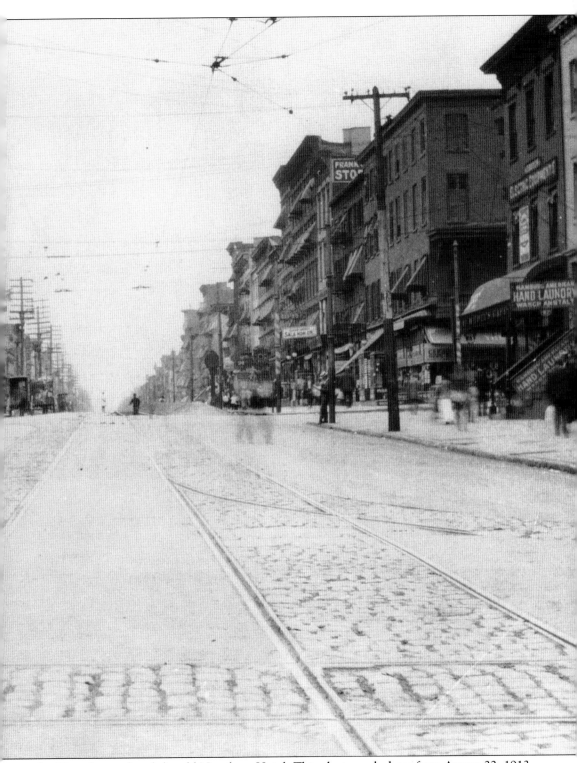

building that replaced the old Napoleon Hotel. This photograph dates from August 22, 1913.
(Ira Deutsch Collection, North Jersey Railway Historical Society.)

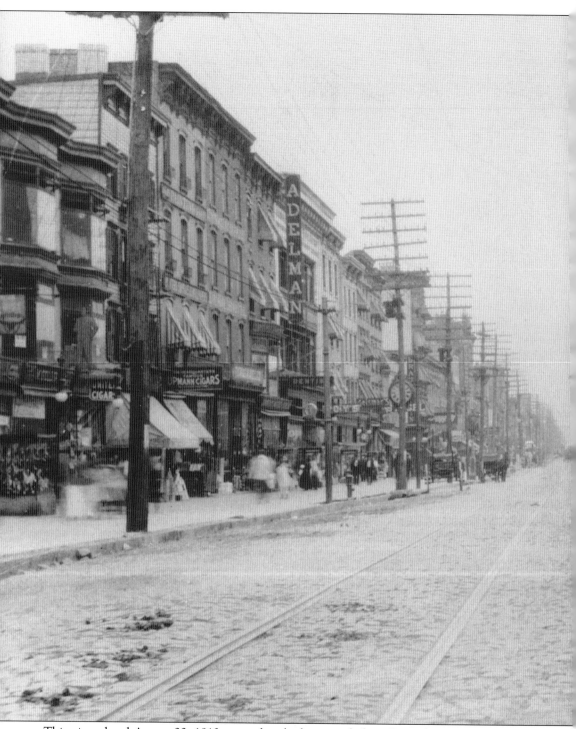

This view, dated August 22, 1913, was taken looking north from Second Street. (Ira Deutsch

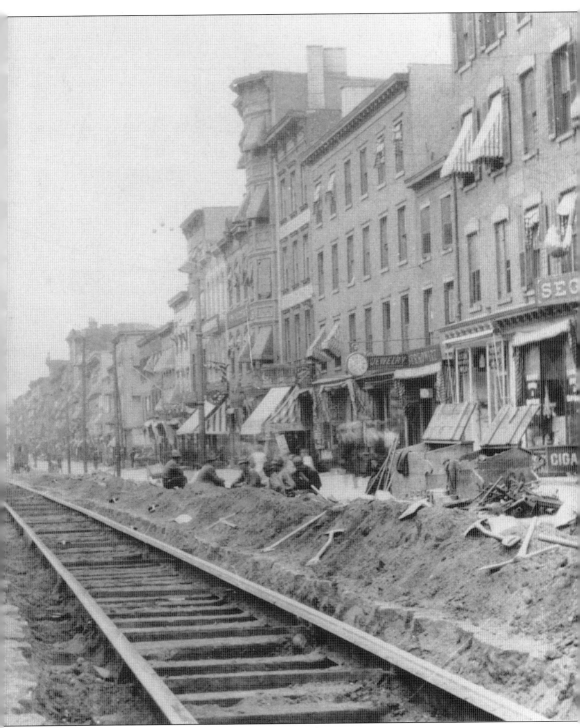

Collection, North Jersey Railway Historical Society.)

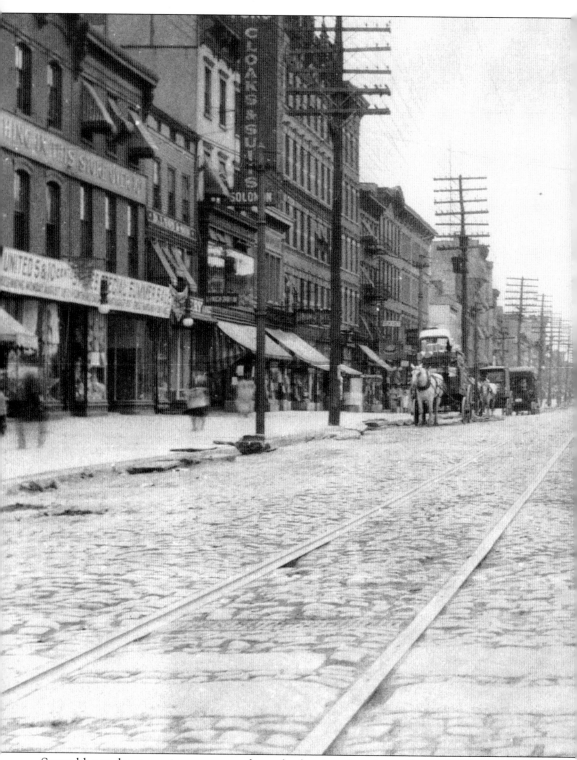

Several horse-drawn carriages are near the curbs, leaving clear the trolley path. This view was taken on Washington Street looking north from Third Street on August 22, 1913. (Ira Deutsch

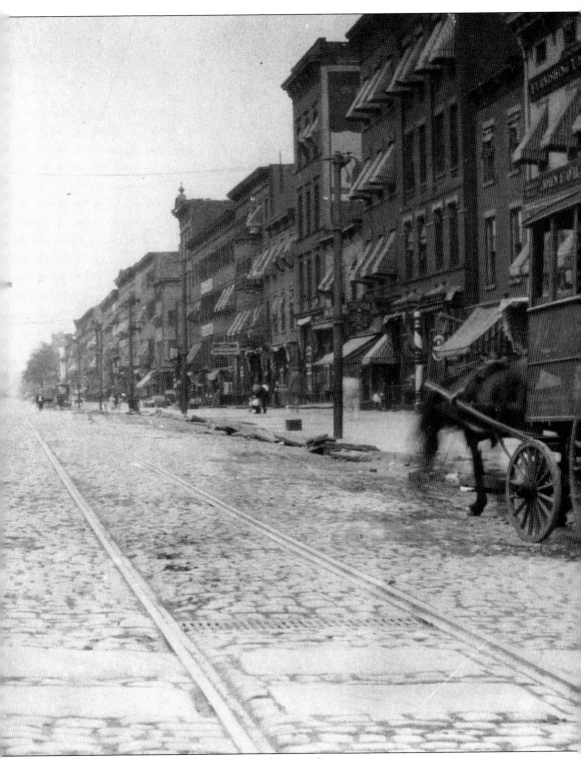

Collection, North Jersey Railway Historical Society.)

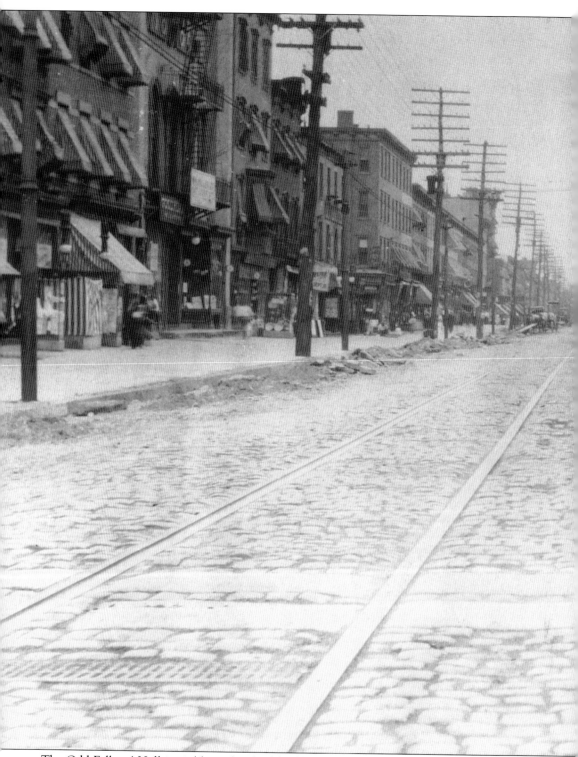

The Odd Fellows' Hall is visible as the third building from the left in this view looking north on Washington Street from Fourth Street on August 22, 1913. (Ira Deutsch Collection, North

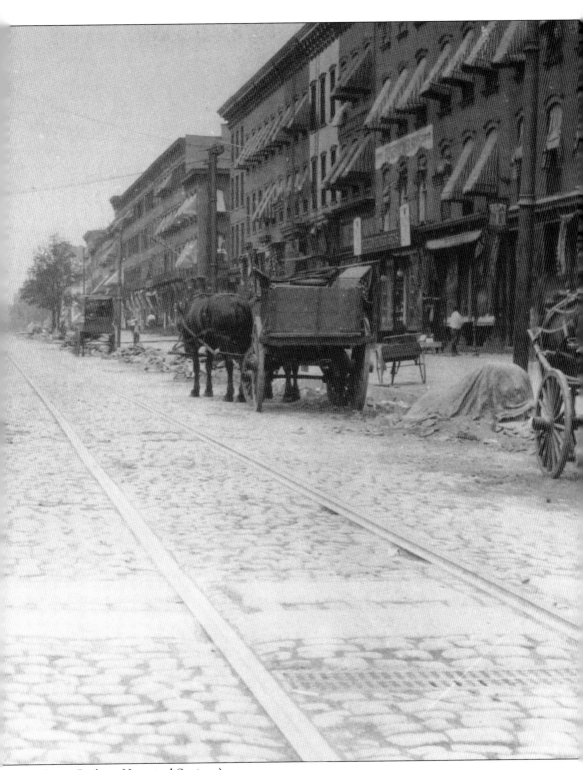

Jersey Railway Historical Society.)

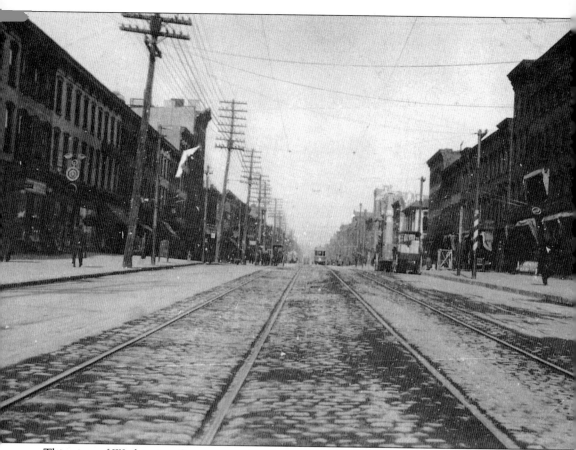

This view of Washington Street was taken from Fifth Street, looking north, on December 20, 1913. (Ira Deutsch Collection, North Jersey Railway Historical Society.)

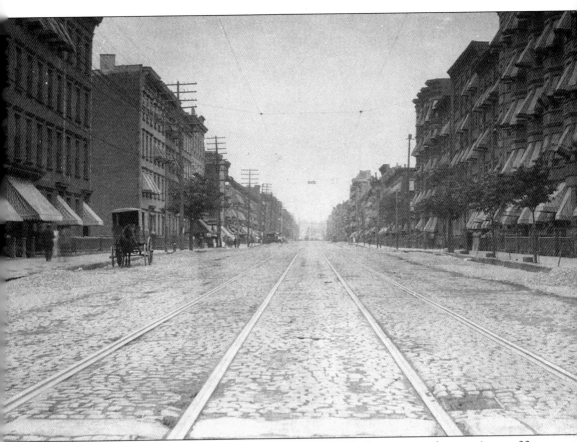

This view, looking north on Washington Street from Eighth Street, was taken on August 22, 1913. (Ira Deutsch Collection, North Jersey Railway Historical Society.)

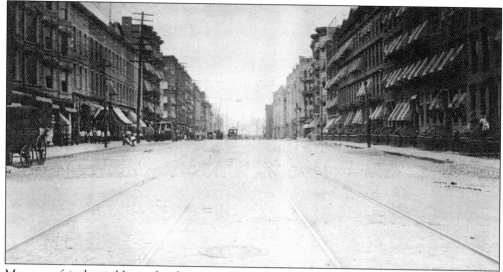

Masts are faintly visible in the distance of the Tietjen and Lang boat repair basin (north of Fourteenth Street) in this view, looking north from Eleventh Street on August 22, 1913. (Ira Deutsch Collection, North Jersey Railway Historical Society.)

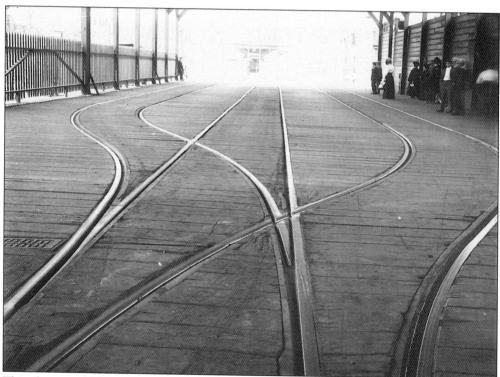

This photograph, documenting the condition of switches and frogs of the trolley tracks at the Fourteenth Street ferry terminal, carries with it a certain beauty and simplicity. Commuters await their trolley cars on either side of the station in this photograph dated May 17, 1914. (Ira Deutsch Collection, North Jersey Railway Historical Society.)

Five

OF FLEETING ELYSIUM

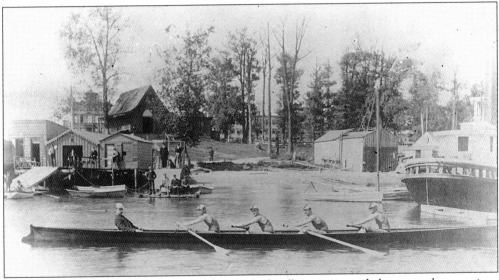

Hoboken's waterfront is the area that has undoubtedly experienced the most changes since the city was first mapped by Colonel John Stevens in 1804. A waterfront park was dedicated between Fourth and Fifth Streets, which is today's Hudson Square Park. Areas for recreation, strolling, boating, and sport (including the first organized game of baseball) were plentiful in the Elysian Fields, a wooded promenade extending to Twelfth Street, with a colonnaded pavilion at its terminus. In the 1866 book *The Hudson, from the Wilderness to the Sea*, Benson J. Lossing bemoaned the loss of the "stately trees near the bank of the river," stating: "All is now changed: the trips of Charon to the Elysian Fields are suspended, and the grounds, stripped of many of the noble trees, have become 'private,' and subjected to the manipulation of the 'real estate agent.' " With the advent of transatlantic shipping in 1863, commerce took precedence over the most recreational uses of the waterfront. This chapter will focus on the appearance and activities of the waterfront of the late 19th century. In this view, looking west toward Tenth Street, uniformed members of a sculling club pass the clubhouse of the New Jersey Yacht Club and other boathouses. (Willenborg Family Collection, courtesy *Hoboken Almanac*, copyright Benedict J. Fernandez.)

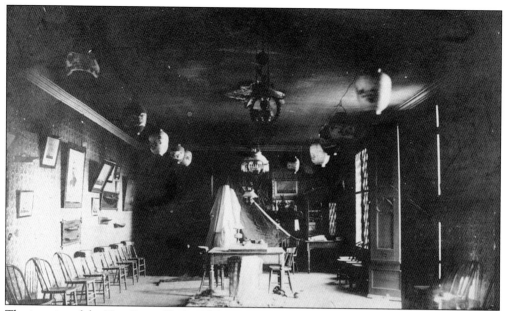

The interior of the New Jersey Yacht Club reveals an ample meeting table and numerous chairs and paintings. The Gothic-styled clubhouse dates from 1845, originally built by the New York Yacht Club. When that club relocated to Staten Island, the New Jersey Yacht Club occupied this clubhouse in 1875. (Courtesy Hoboken Public Library.)

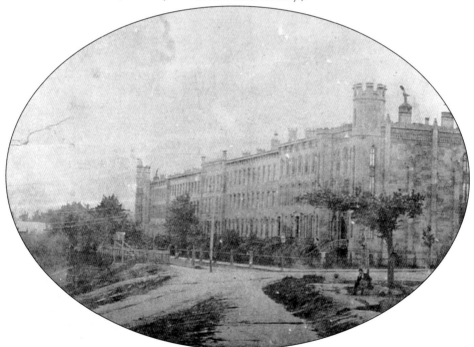

The crenelated turrets of Franklin Terrace, which was the 1850s residential block occupying River and Hudson Streets (between Second and Third Streets), is seen in this 1880s view looking south. Fairly steep paths lead towards River Walk, the Elysian Fields, and the docks. (Courtesy Hoboken Public Library.)

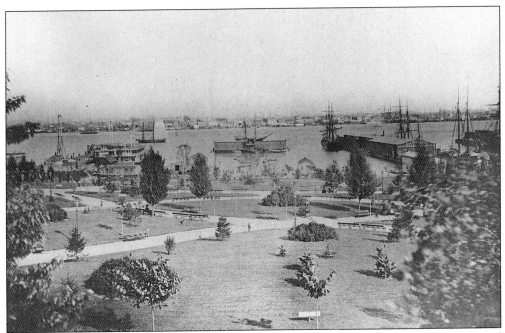

This tranquil view, thought to date from the 1870s, shows recreational boating clubs and yacht builders with the pier and dock of the Baltic Lloyd Line to the right. Most of the boats visible are under sail. (Willenborg Family Collection, courtesy *Hoboken Almanac*, copyright Benedict J. Fernandez.)

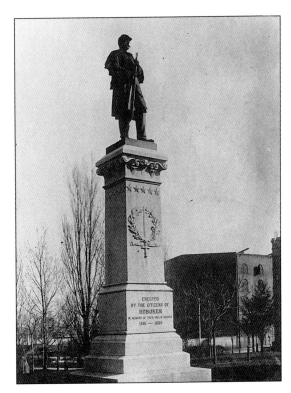

The Civil War Monument was erected in Hudson Square Park. In this photograph, the Campbell Storage Warehouse is visible to the right, as is the corner turret of the Franklin Terrace block. (Willenborg Family Collection, courtesy *Hoboken Almanac*, copyright Benedict J. Fernandez.)

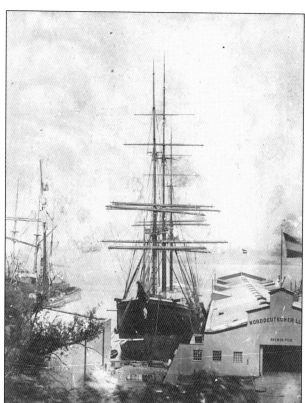

A tall-masted transatlantic ship is seen here from River Street at its dock at the North German Lloyd pier. (Courtesy Hoboken Public Library.)

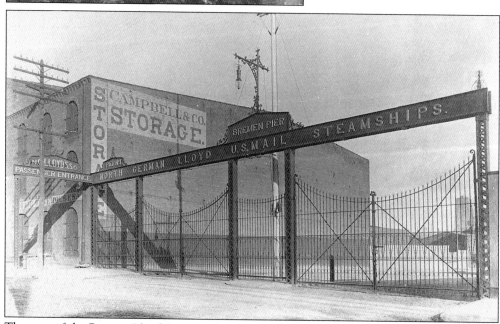

The gate of the Bremen Lloyd Lines on River Street is captured here at a quiet time in which one can appreciate the depth of the Campbell Warehouse building. There were once two Campbell storehouses, one at Fourth Street and the other at Sixth Street. (Willenborg Family Collection, courtesy *Hoboken Almanac*, copyright Benedict J. Fernandez.)

This beautifully engraved invitation announces the inspection of the North German Lloyd steamship *Saale* in 1886. (Courtesy Hoboken Public Library.)

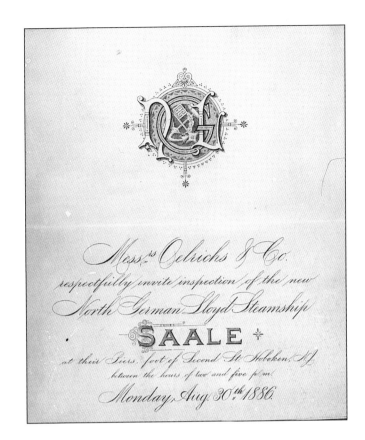

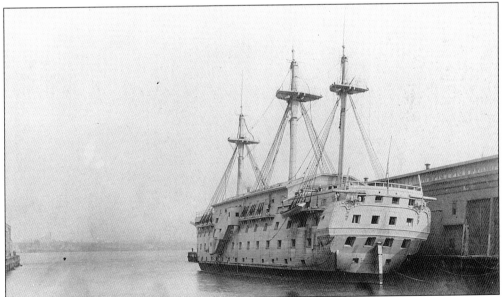

The square-rigged *Portsmouth* was used as a training ship for naval reserves during the Spanish-American War. Two guns were removed from this ship in 1906 and placed on either side of the Soldier's Monument in Hudson Square Park. (Willenborg Family Collection, courtesy *Hoboken Almanac*, copyright Benedict J. Fernandez.)

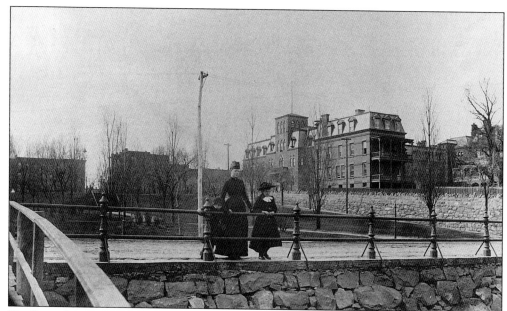

Strollers who ventured down to promenade along the waterfront were likely to see both commercial and recreational activity coexist. In this view, the Stevens Institute Administration Building is to the right. (Willenborg Family Collection, courtesy *Hoboken Almanac*, copyright Benedict J. Fernandez.)

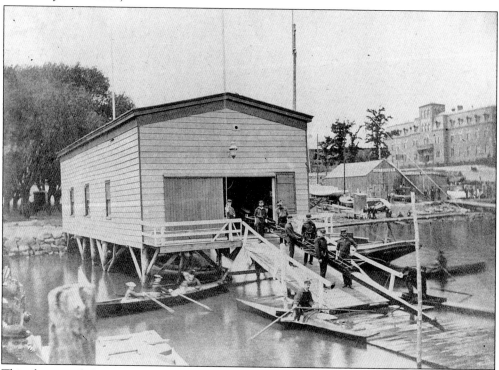

This photograph from an earlier time shows a six-man rowing group about to put their boat into the water as a boat carrying three ladies approaches. (Willenborg Family Collection, courtesy *Hoboken Almanac*, copyright Benedict J. Fernandez.)

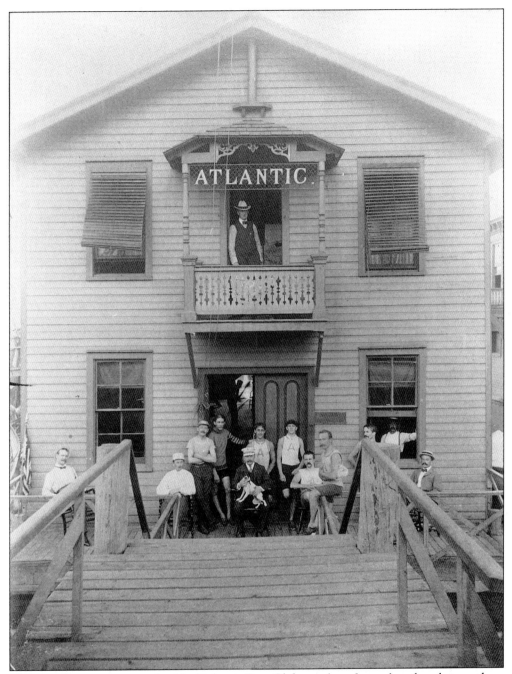

This casual group photograph of the Atlantic Boat Club members shows the relaxed atmosphere of a carefree afternoon. The Atlantics fought to maintain their presence on the waterfront and successfully sued in 1909. Theirs was the last boat club to remain along Hoboken's waterfront. (Willenborg Family Collection, courtesy *Hoboken Almanac*, copyright Benedict J. Fernandez.)

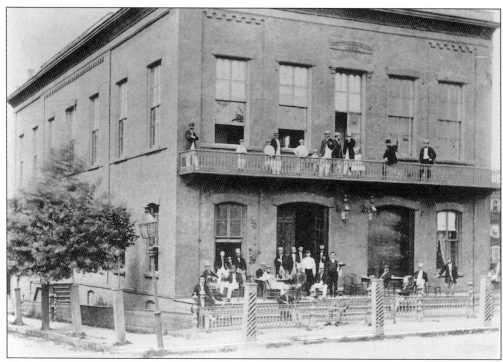

The German Club (later known as the Union Club) on Hudson and Sixth Streets, was the center of social activity for the German community. This photograph shows the club before expansions were constructed to the north. (Courtesy Hoboken Public Library.)

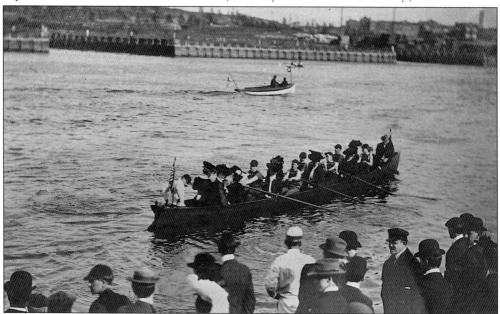

This scene captures the merriment of a rowing club regatta, in which club members would venture onto the river with their guests. The exertion evident in the rowers contrasts with the tranquil elegance of their guests. (Willenborg Family Collection, courtesy *Hoboken Almanac*, copyright Benedict J. Fernandez.)

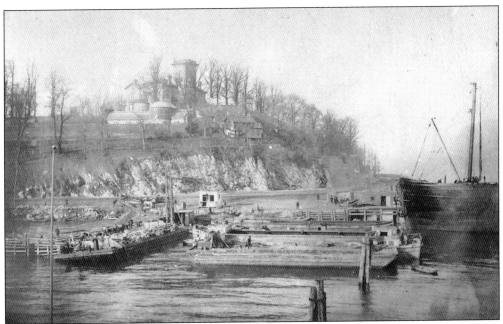

The Stevens Castle landmark, with its greenhouses and various outbuildings, is visible at the top of the hill. It rises 100 feet above the river and is the highest point in Hoboken, set atop a deposit of serpentine rock. In the foreground, loaded barges rest at the docks. (Courtesy Hoboken Public Library.)

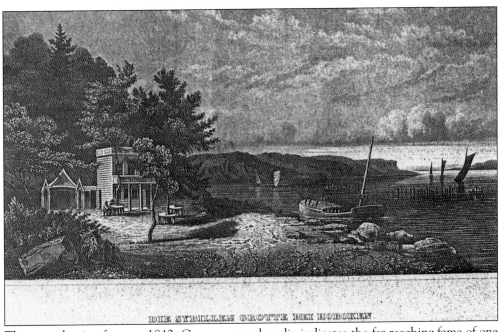

DIE SYBILLEN GROTTE BEI HOBOKEN

This reproduction from an 1840s German encyclopedia indicates the far-reaching fame of one of the attractions of Elysian Fields and its River Walk. The attraction is Sybil's Cave, a natural spring enclosed by the pillared entrance to the left in this engraving. It was opened in 1836, when Colonel Stevens also planted trees along the riverfront. (Author's collection.)

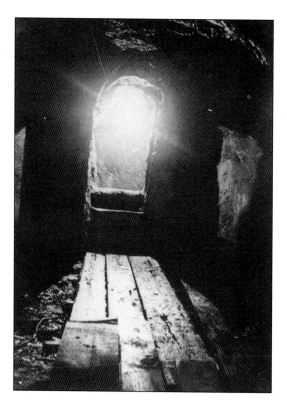

This unusual view, taken from within Sybil's Cave in the 1930s, shows the planks on the floor and hewed-rock ceiling. The cave is now totally sealed but would make a worthwhile public archeology study. (Courtesy Hoboken Public Library.)

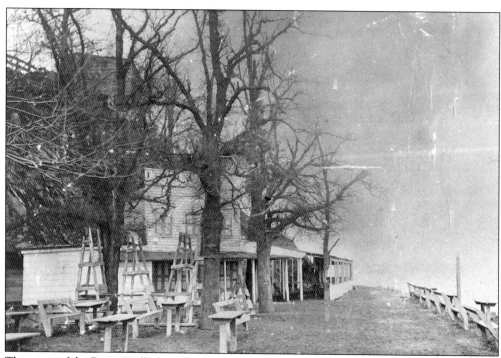

This view of the River Walk shows Sybil's Cave shuttered for cold weather. (Courtesy Hoboken Public Library.)

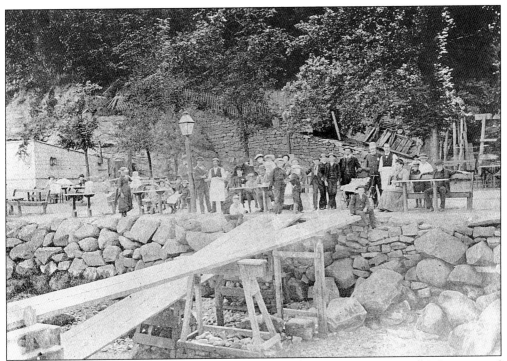

A mid-summer scene near Sybil's Cave in the 1880s finds families enjoying mineral waters and refreshments while watching the passing scenes on the river. (Willenborg Family Collection, courtesy *Hoboken Almanac*, copyright Benedict J. Fernandez.)

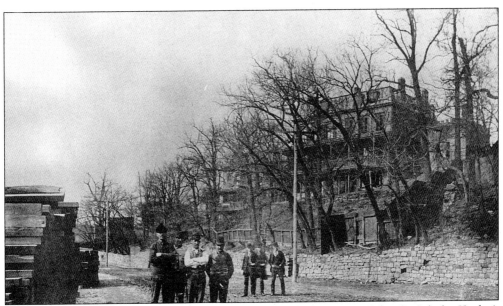

A group of workmen stand on River Walk in the lumber section of the C. Schultz Yard. A Stevens Institute dormitory is in the background of this image. (Willenborg Family Collection, courtesy *Hoboken Almanac*, copyright Benedict J. Fernandez.)

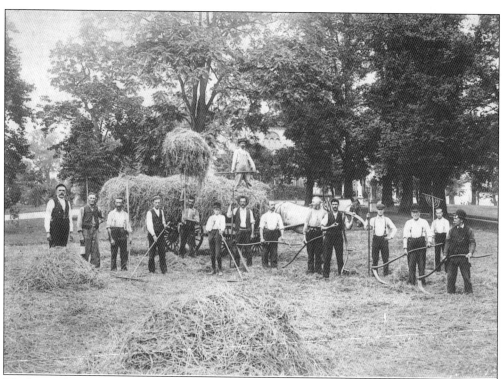

The hay gatherers on the Stevens Estate in the 1880s suggest a rural, rather than urban setting. The Stevens Castle is in the background of this photograph taken by Hoboken resident B.F. Barries.

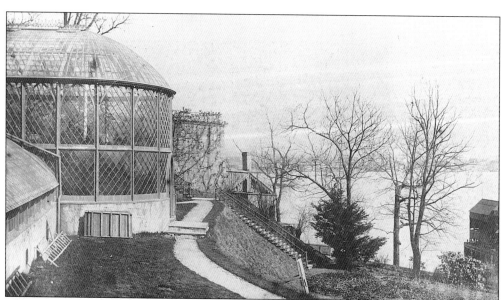

This view, taken from the south side of Stevens Castle, shows the south side of the conservatory and the wonderful vantage point enjoyed by the property. A steep stairway leads down to a flower bed. (Willenborg Family Collection, courtesy *Hoboken Almanac*, copyright Benedict J. Fernandez.)

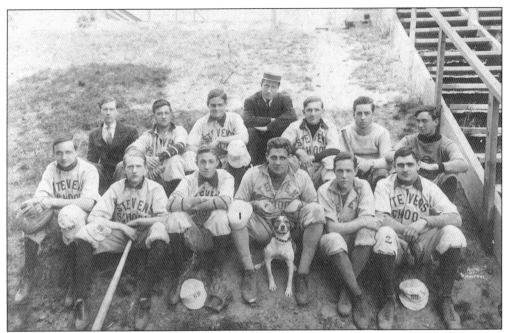

The baseball team of the Stevens Prep School, on the Stevens Campus, posed for this group picture with Coach Saunders. Storie Schultze is in the center with the mascot. (Courtesy Hoboken Public Library.)

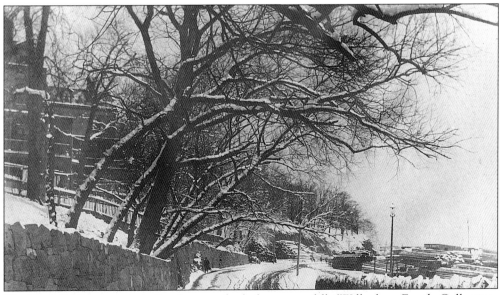

The River Walk was artistically photographed after a snowfall. (Willenborg Family Collection, courtesy *Hoboken Almanac*, copyright Benedict J. Fernandez.)

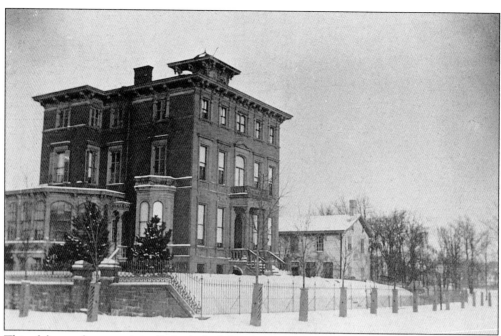

This elaborate house, originally built for John Crusius, and later occupied by Laurance Fagan, was located at Tenth and Hudson Streets. The barn to the rear of the property was used by the original owner to raise a prize breed of chickens. This house, no longer standing, once looked out upon the old yacht clubhouse. (Willenborg Family Collection, courtesy *Hoboken Almanac*, copyright Benedict J. Fernandez.)

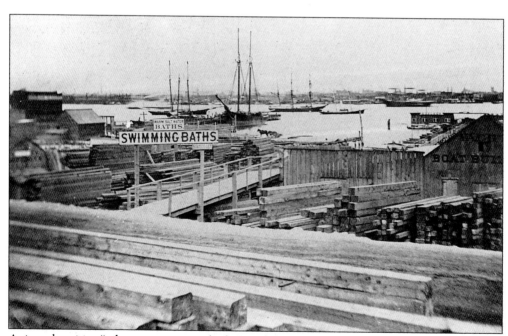

A sign advertising "salt water swimming baths" can be seen amid stacks of lumber at the waterfront. (Willenborg Family Collection, courtesy *Hoboken Almanac*, copyright Benedict J. Fernandez.)

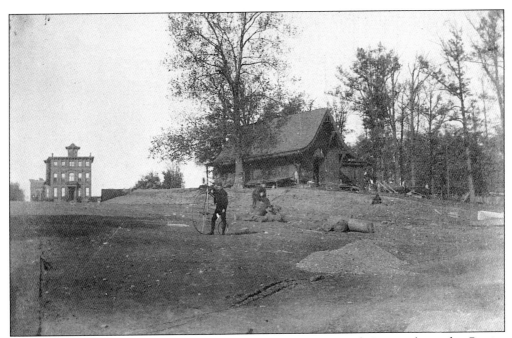

This view, looking west from the banks of the Hudson near Tenth Street, shows the Crusius house to the left and the old New York Yacht Club to the right. The Rosedale Boat Club later occupied a cove near Tenth Street after the removal of the Gothic-styled building in 1885. (Willenborg Family Collection, courtesy *Hoboken Almanac*, copyright Benedict J. Fernandez.)

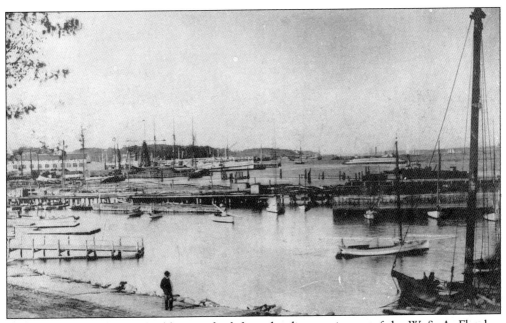

In this view *c.* 1890s, the building to the left in the distance is part of the W. & A. Fletcher Iron Works, on the waterfront between Twelfth and Fourteenth Streets. (Courtesy Hoboken Public Library.)

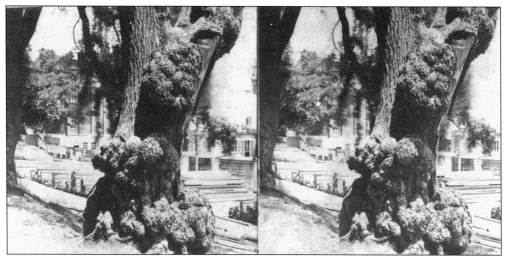

An aged willow tree along the river was the subject of a stereoscopic card in the late 1890s. When viewed in a special viewer, a three-dimensional effect was achieved, which must have been striking with the bulbous formations in the trunk of this tree. (Courtesy Hoboken Public Library.)

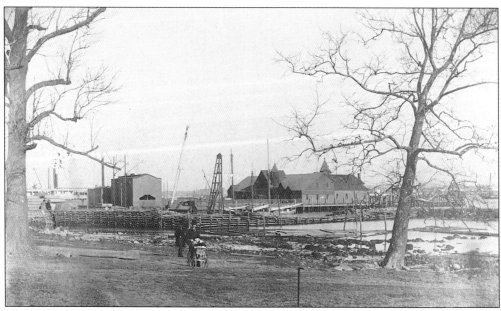

The gables and peaked roof of the Fourteenth Street ferryhouse are seen in the center of this photograph, looking northeast from the south. The gravel path along the river is traversed by two strollers, one of which is pushing a baby carriage. (Willenborg Family Collection, courtesy *Hoboken Almanac*, copyright Benedict J. Fernandez.)

A crew member from J.P. Morgan's yacht *Corsair III*, prepares the mast for revarnishing. The yacht was designed by John Beavor-Webb, and built in 1899 by T.S. Marvel & Sons at Newburgh, N.Y., with an engine and boilers manufactured by W. & A. Fletcher Company, Hoboken. The yacht was often docked on the Hoboken side of the Hudson, opposite the New York Yacht Club landing, when not in Europe or near Mr. Morgan's country home, "Cragston." (Courtesy Keystone-Mast Collection UCR/California Museum of Photography, University of California, Riverside, Neg. #X9143.)

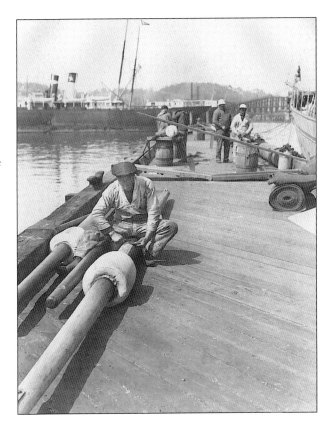

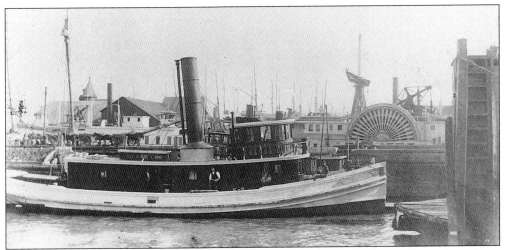

The riverfront ship repair and dry-dock company, Tietjen & Lang, is shown here looking south from Fifteenth Street. This view shows the ongoing activities evident by ferryhouse, in the distance to the left, and the steam-powered tugboat in the foreground. Visible to the right is an enormous sidewheel of the type seen in the 1860 birds-eye view of Hoboken (page 6). That vented type of wheelbox was superseded by the semi-enclosed ones popular in the early 1900s. (Willenborg Family Collection, courtesy *Hoboken Almanac*, copyright Benedict J. Fernandez.)

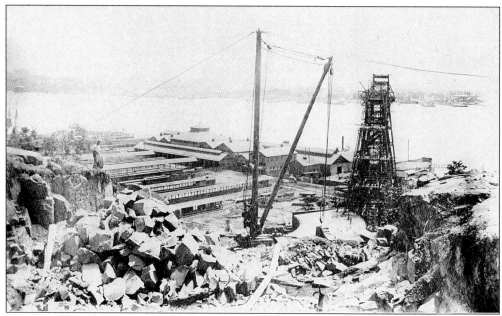

In the cove north of Hoboken, 100 feet east of the Palisades, the North River Railroad built an amazing structure designed to lift rail cars up and west to the El Dorado amusement park. (Willenborg Family Collection, courtesy *Hoboken Almanac*, copyright Benedict J. Fernandez.)

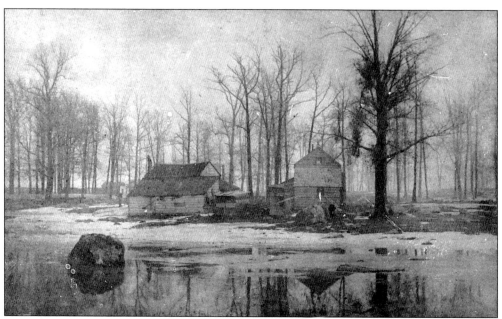

These shanties were used by shad fishermen and were located in the Weehawken Cove north of Hoboken. One Monmouth County individual, Captain Samuel Ludlow, maintained nets and a fishery variously described as Hoboken and Weehawken. He anticipated enjoying the first shad around St. Patrick's Day. This misty and icy setting could very well have been photographed in the month of March. (Courtesy Hoboken Public Library.)

Six

THE CHANGING WATERFRONT

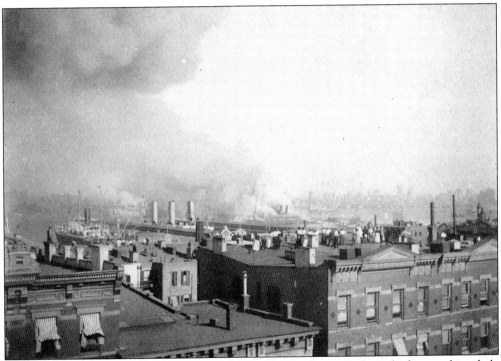

Residents gathered on a Hudson Street rooftop to observe the tragic fire, which started in a bale of cotton and spread rapidly through an opened shutter at the Campbell storehouse. The fire, which took the lives of over 200 people, took five days to extinguish. In the aftermath of the fire, Hoboken's business interests, organized into a Board of Trade by 1904, sought to extend the pierhead lines to benefit commerce. With extended piers a reality within the next decade, the waterfront became almost totally industrialized, except for the Atlantic Club boathouse, which was dwarfed by its neighbors. Notwithstanding these improvements, the advent of WW I deeply affected Hoboken. This chapter will look at some of the changes brought to the waterfront in the 20th century. (Courtesy Hoboken Public Library.)

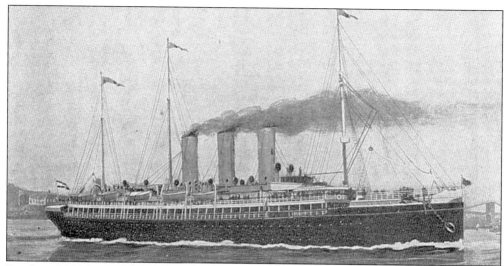

By the 1890s, several transatlantic shipping companies were firmly established along the Hoboken waterfront. These included the Netherlands-American Steam Navigation Company, whose pier and dock were at the foot of 50th Street; the Thingvalla Steamship Company, at the foot of Fourth Street; and the Wilson Line, on River Street between Second and Third Streets. The North German Lloyd Steamship Company was based at the foot of Third Street. The Hamburg-America Packet Company introduced a new service in the 1890s, featuring a twin-screw system. This photograph of the twin-screw steamer *Columbia* appeared in the book, *The Evening News and Hoboken*, 1893.

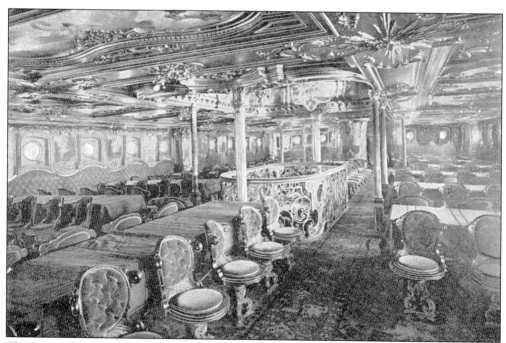

This view of the main saloon of the first cabin of the *Columbia* shows the opulence of the décor, reflecting the newly attained levels of comfort and elegance comparable to those found in a first-class hotel. (*The Evening News and Hoboken*.)

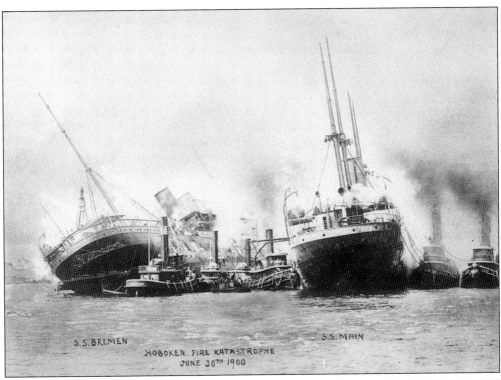

S.S. BREMEN   S.S. MAIN

HOBOKEN FIRE KATASTROPHE
JUNE 30TH 1900

This view was taken from the water of the liners SS *Bremen* (to the left) and the SS *Main* (to the right) during the enormous pier fire of June 30, 1900. Tug boats and nine fireboats were engaged in fighting the blaze. (Courtesy Hoboken Public Library.)

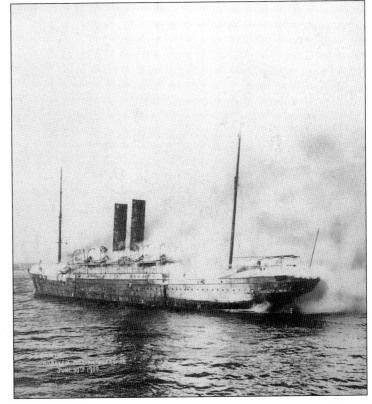

The SS *Saale* is burning in this photograph of the June 30th fire. (Courtesy Hoboken Public Library.)

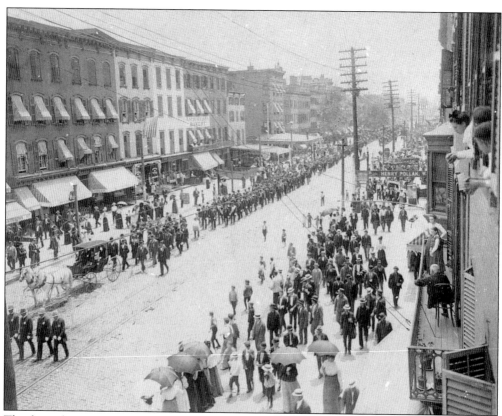

The funeral procession for the dock fire victims made its way down Washington Street; then, the dead were interred in a separate grave area at the Flower Hill Cemetery in North Bergen. (Courtesy Hoboken Public Library.)

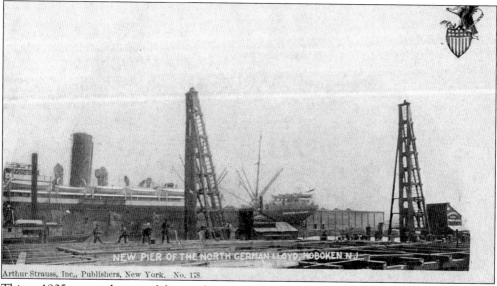

This *c.* 1905 postcard view celebrates the construction of the North German Lloyd's new pier. (Author's collection.)

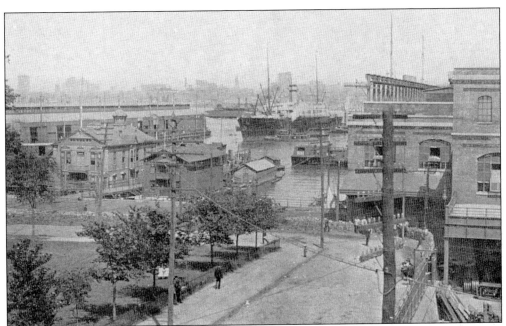

This postcard view, published by E.F. Walter and entitled "docking a liner," shows boathouses dwarfed by the nearby piers. The boathouse of the Valencia boat club is to the left. (Author's collection.)

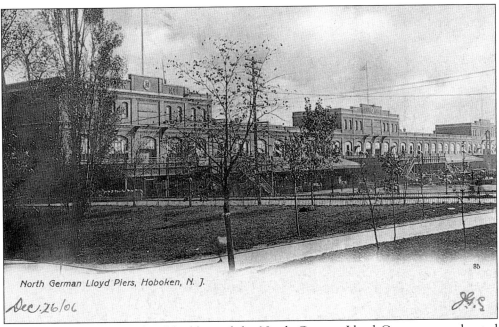

North German Lloyd Piers, Hoboken, N. J.

Dec. 26/06

The completed brick pierhead building of the North German Lloyd Company was located on River Street between Second and Fourth Streets, seen here in this 1905 postcard view. (Author's collection.)

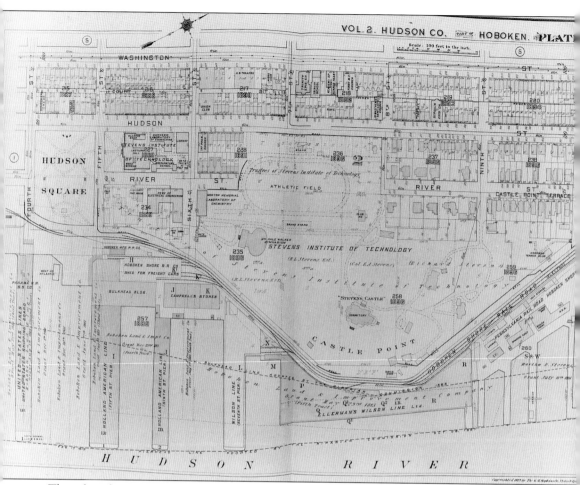

This plate from a 1923 Hudson County atlas indicates by dotted lines the many leases and grants issued by the Hoboken Land and Improvement Company. Also of note are the bulkhead extensions, under the jurisdiction of the Riparian Commission, the New Jersey Harbor Commission, and the New York Harbor Line Board. Hoboken's commercial interests had petitioned the Harbor Commission for permission to extend the piers to the extent of those on the New York side. Concerns about extended piers being a danger to navigation by creating "impediments to the fairway" were tempered with the need to accommodate the increasing length of oceanliners. The tracks of the Shore Manufacturer's Railroad provided direct access for manufacturers to the pier storage warehouses that linked to seven different rail lines. The boathouse of the Atlantic Rowing Club (directly east of Hudson Square park) was the lone survivor of the clubs. (G.M. Hopkins Atlas, Stevens Family Papers Collection, New Jersey Historical Commission.)

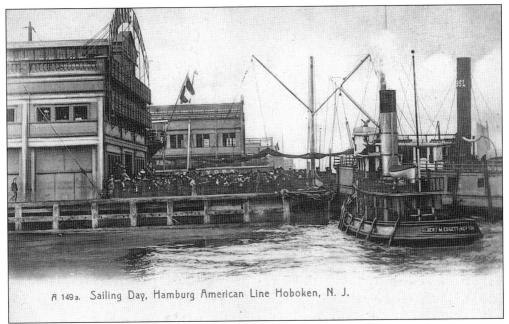

A 149a. Sailing Day, Hamburg American Line Hoboken, N. J.

This postcard view depicts the excitement of "sailing day" on the Hamburg-American Line pier. (Author's collection.)

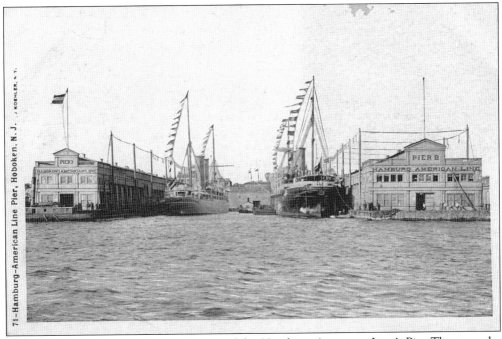

This view from the river gives a glimpse of the Hamburg-American Line's Pier Three, to the left, and Pier Two, to the right, with liners in their berths. The tall masts indicate that ships still relied upon wind-power to augment their engine-power. (Author's collection.)

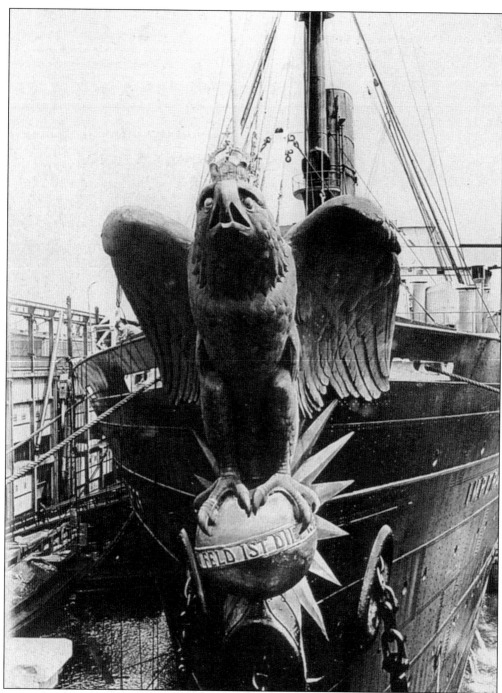

Pier extensions, granted in 1913, began at the Sixth Street pier at Hoboken and extended south to South Street in Jersey City and allowed ample length to accommodate the *Imperator*, heralded as a "marine wonder of modern times." The *Imperator* was the first of three sister ships, the other two being the *Vaterland* and the *Bismarck*, which represented advances in marine construction and safety. This close-up of the enormous figurehead was taken at Hoboken's Second Street pier. (HAPAG Archives, courtesy John Maxtone-Graham.)

The *Imperator* represented a new standard of elegance in oceanliner design. This elegant vestibule led to the social hall. (HAPAG Archives, courtesy John Maxtone-Graham.)

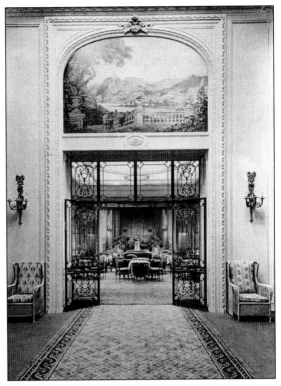

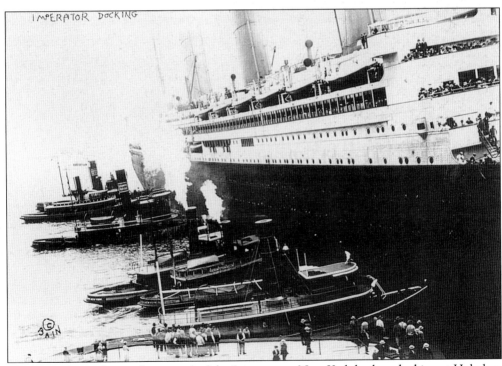

This view shows the maiden arrival of the *Imperator* to New York harbor, docking at Hoboken in June of 1913. (HAPAG Archives, courtesy John Maxtone-Graham.)

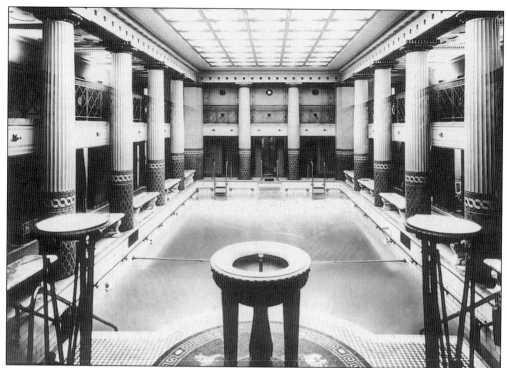

The *Imperator* featured this interior swimming pool, which was inspired by interior designer Charles Mewés. He had first created a "Pompeian Bath" facility for the Royal Automobile Club in London. (HAPAG Archives, courtesy John Maxtone-Graham.)

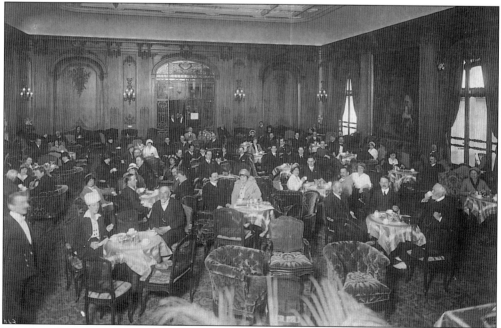

The first-class main lounge, with its elegantly paneled interior and dome of leaded glass, was also known as the social hall. (HAPAG Archives, courtesy John Maxtone-Graham.)

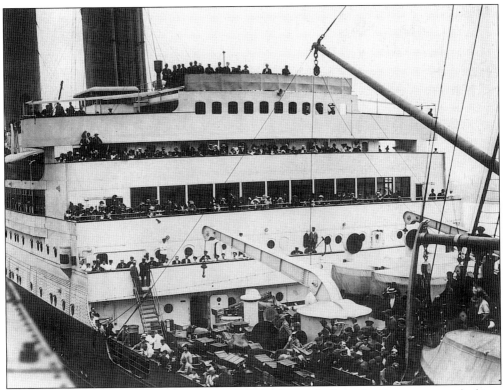

A sea of luggage of all three classes occupied the lower deck as the *Imperator* was docking. (HAPAG Archives, courtesy John Maxtone-Graham.)

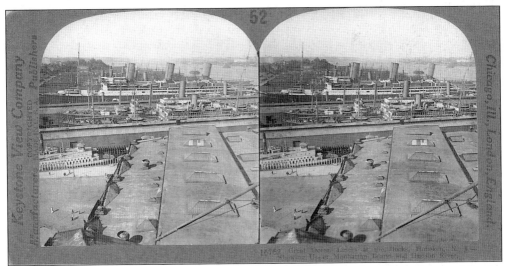

This stereoscopic view, dated 1915, shows the German steamship lines' vessels, seized by the U.S. government in 1914. The *Imperator* remained in port in Europe, but the *Vaterland* was renamed the *Leviathan*. (Keystone View Company, author's collection.)

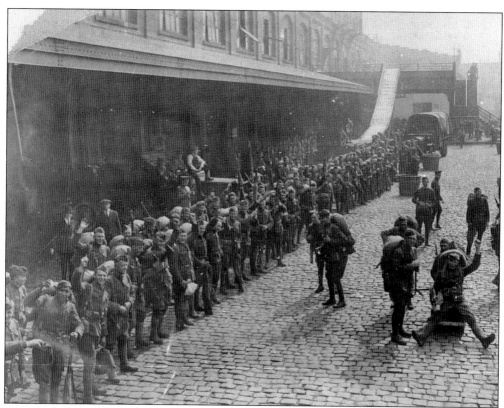

After Hoboken became a port of embarkation for servicemen, "Heaven, Hell, or Hoboken" became a popular expression. Here, doughboys pausing in front of the piers prepare to board the SS *President Grant* for Coblentz. (Courtesy Hoboken Public Library.)

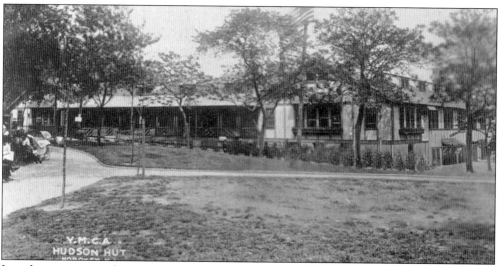

In order to accommodate the enormous number of enlisted men, who were passing through the port of Hoboken during WW I, the "Hudson Hut" was constructed on the site of the present Little League field. (Author's collection.)

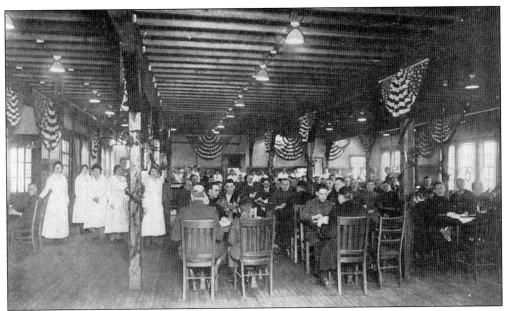

A commodious cafeteria was staffed largely by volunteer workers who fed and tried to lift the morale of the soldiers, so many of whom had come from all parts of the country. (Author's collection.)

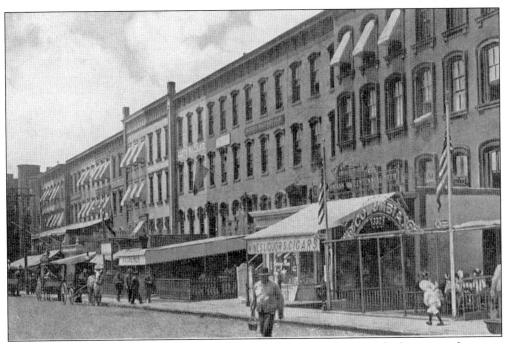

The once-picturesque terraces of River and Hudson Streets had become the locations of taverns, given their proximity to the piers. Shortly after the outbreak of war, the U.S. War Department ordered the closure of over 200 bars in Hoboken. (Author's collection.)

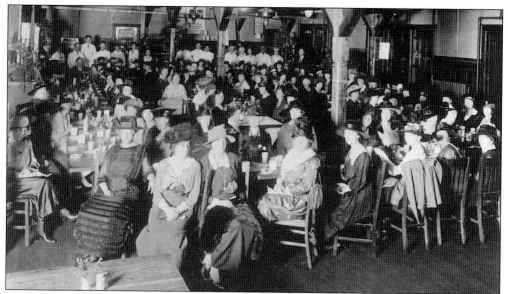

This gathering of volunteer workers at the Hudson Hut underscores the large number of people needed to carry on the work accomplished there. (Author's collection.)

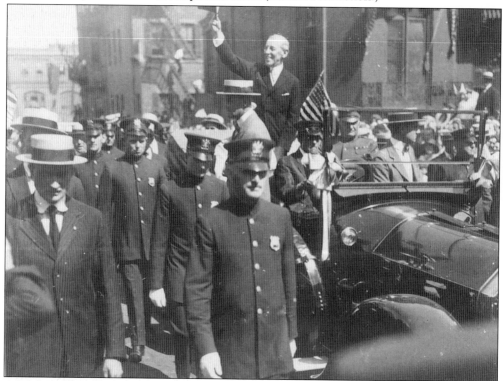

A jubilant celebration accompanied the return of President and Mrs. Wilson after they returned from Verseilles, France. President Wilson is seen here in an open car in a motorcade with Mrs. Wilson, General Shanks, and others between Hudson and Washington Streets. The Wilsons departed from the Hoboken piers en route to the White House on July 8, 1919. (Courtesy Hoboken Public Library, gift of Dave Hamilton.)

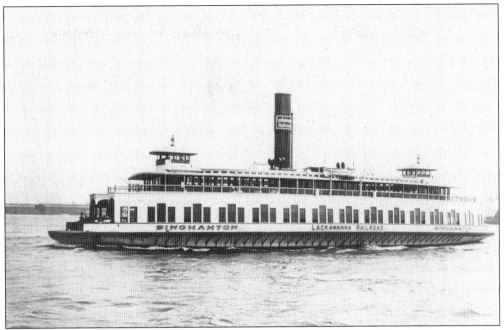

Starting on May 15, 1918, Hoboken ferries transported 242,330 officers for embarkation and by December 2, an additional 127,432 officers and men. The largest number of troops transported in one day was 9,803 on August 8, 1919, the day of the Victory Parade in New York City. This ferry, the *Binghamton*, built in 1905, survived the terminal fire of 1905 and is now a restaurant of the same name in Edgewater, New Jersey. (Courtesy Hoboken Public Library.)

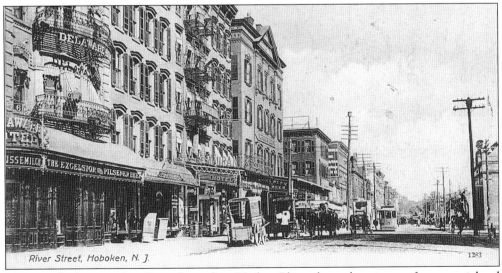

River Street, Hoboken, N. J.

This view, looking north up River Street from Hudson Place, shows the mixture of commercial and industrial establishments concentrated in an area blocks away from residential neighborhoods. (Author's collection.)

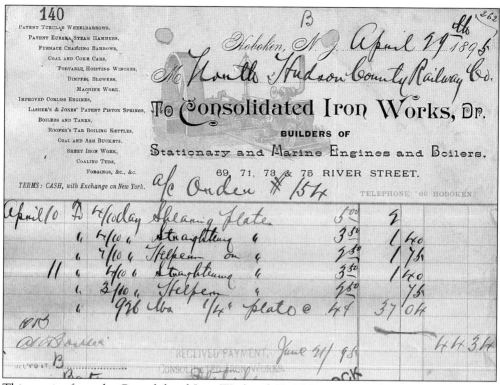

This receipt from the Consolidated Iron Works of 69–75 River Street lists the wide range of equipment manufactured there. In addition to stationary marine engines and boilers, were steam hammers, furnace-charging barrows, and improved Corliss engines. (Author's collection.)

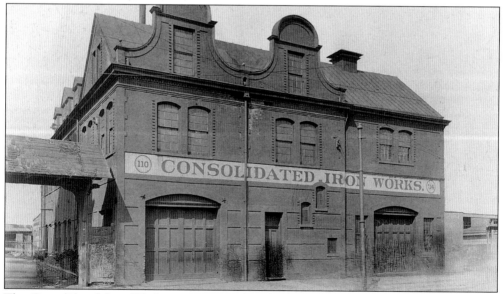

The Consolidated Iron Works was associated with the W. & A. Fletcher Company, which relocated to Hoboken from lower Manhattan in 1890. This photograph depicts the River Street Iron Works. (Hagley Museum and Library.)

Prior to relocating to Hoboken in 1890, the North River Iron Works was located at Vestry and West Streets in New York City. A successor firm of the H.R. Dunham & Company Archimedes Works, the company was formed by brothers Andrew and William Fletcher and J.G. Harrison in 1853. The company began doing repair work and later specialized in the manufacture of marine engines, in particular, the vertical, walking-beam engines. An air pump chamber for a sidewheeler is seen in this image on the sidewalk at its New York facility. (Hagley Museum and Library.)

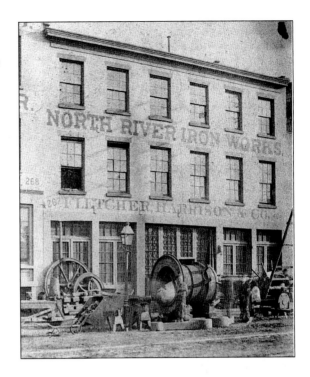

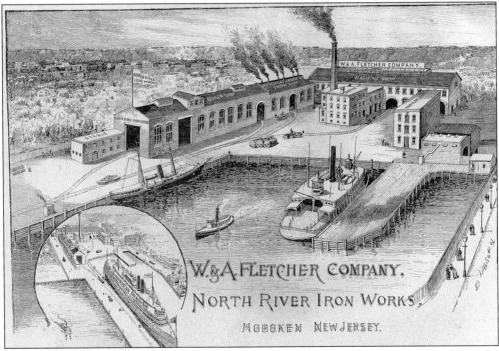

This engraved presentation appeared in *The Evening News and Hoboken* in 1893. It shows the orientation of the buildings, including the boiler shop (in the foreground to the left), the smith shop (west of the boiler shop), and the machine shop (along Hudson Street from Twelfth to Fourteenth Streets).

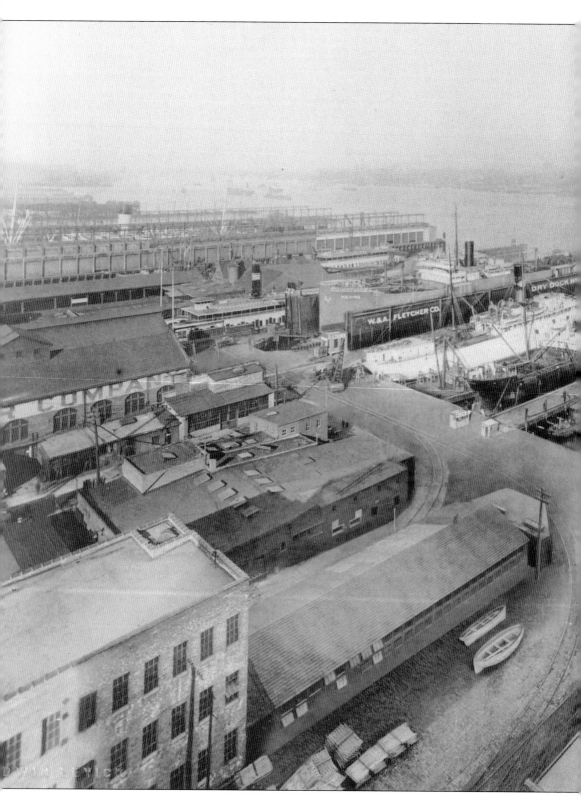

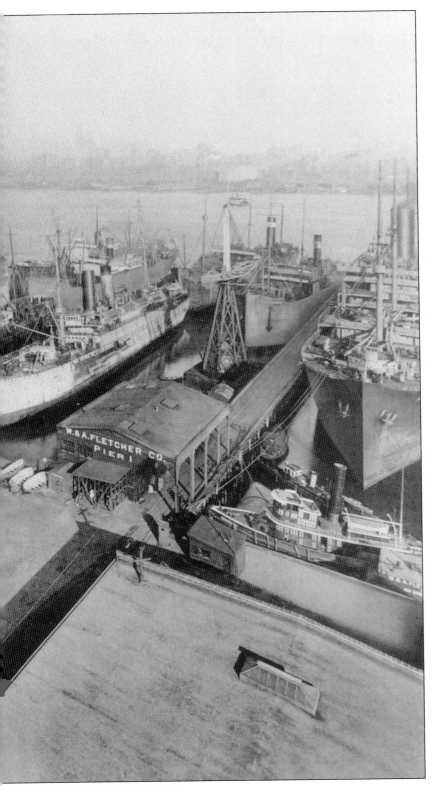

This impressive view shows the operation of the W. & A. Fletcher Company and North River Iron Works, which was responsible for building many of the largest steamships, steamboats, and steam yachts in the country. The company built the *Governor Cobb* for the Eastern Steamship Company and the *Yale* and *Harvard*, which were the first turbine steamships built in America, for the Metropolitan Steamship Company. The company also constructed the yacht *Corsair*, owned by J. Pierpont Morgan. (Hagley Museum and Library.)

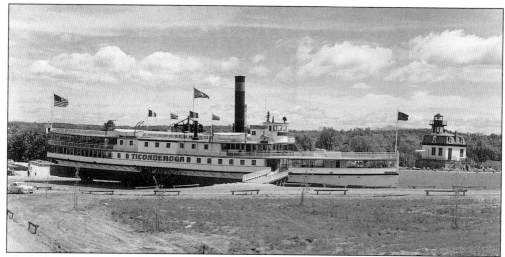

The W. & A. Fletcher Company manufactured the boilers, engine controls, and supervised the construction of the steel hull of the 1905 Lake Champlain passenger packet and sidewheel steamboat *Ticonderoga*. At 220 feet long, it is the largest artifact in the Shelburne Museum's fascinating collection of buildings, antiques, and objects representing American art and technology. This photograph dates from 1955, shortly after the ship's overland arrival at the museum, where it was set within a sloping dell. The *Ticonderoga*, designated a National Historic Landmark in 1963, underwent an extensive restoration between 1993 and 1998. Visitors can take a footbridge onto the ship and view informative exhibits throughout the four deck levels and all areas of the restored interior. (Shelburne Museum, Shelburne, Vermont.)

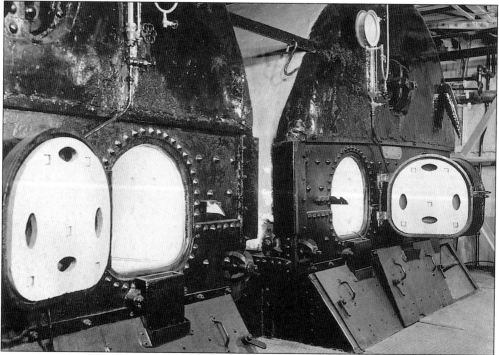

Two massive "fire-tube boilers," each of 750 horsepower, provided steam power for the *Ticonderoga*. (Shelburne Museum, Shelburne, Vermont.)

The wooden cabinet enclosing the "steam chest" of the engine in the control room can be seen from the stateroom deck level. (Shelburne Museum, Shelburne, Vermont.)

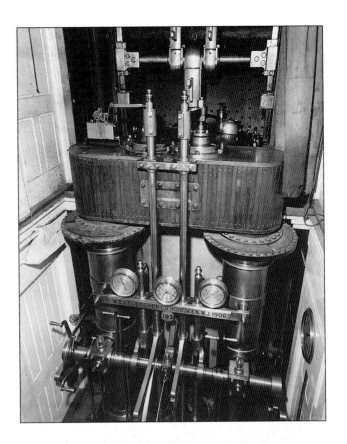

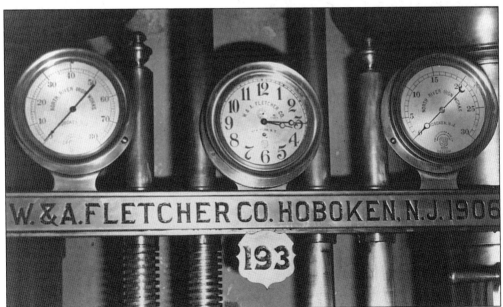

The control gauges identify W. & A. Fletcher Company, Hoboken, as the manufacturer of the *Ticonderoga* engine. The gauges to the left and right identify the allied company North River Iron Works, Hoboken, as well. (Shelburne Museum, Shelburne, Vermont.)

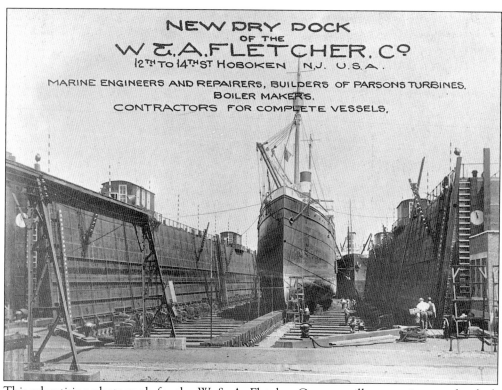

This advertising photograph for the W. & A. Fletcher Company illustrates its new dry-dock facility. The still and deep harbor made Hoboken's waterfront ideal for these types of vessels. (Hagley Museum and Library.)

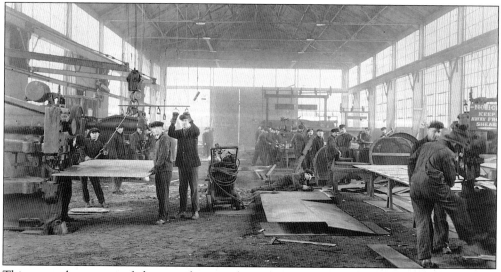

This unusual sequence of photographs was taken when laborers were at work in various shops, either under W. & A. Fletcher or the successor firm, United Dry Docks. This is a view of the metalwork shop. (Hagley Museum and Library.)

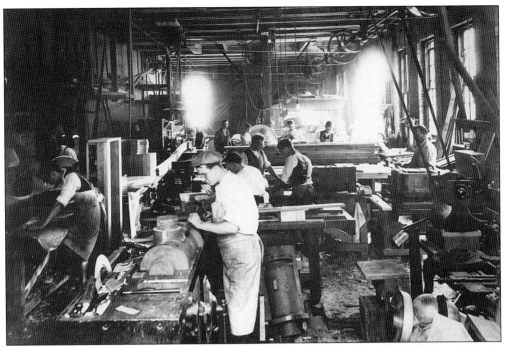

This undated photograph is a view of the carpentry shop. (Hagley Museum and Library.)

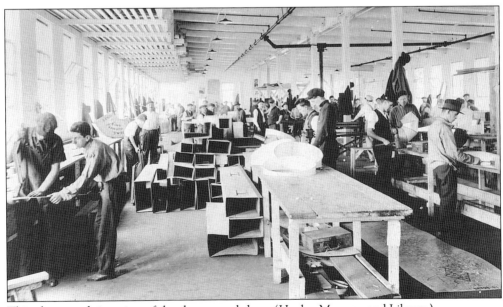

This photograph is a view of the sheet metal shop. (Hagley Museum and Library.)

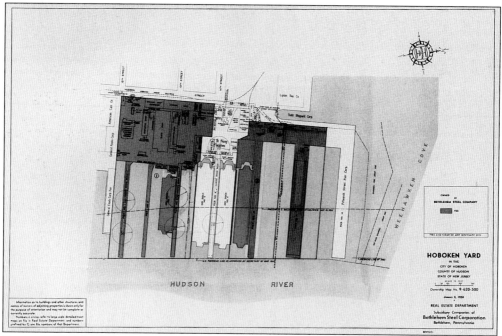

During WW I the W. & A. Fletcher Company was primarily occupied by converting ships for troop transport service. The company specialized in repair work after the war, becoming United Dry Docks Inc. in 1929. When Bethlehem Steel purchased United Dry Docks in 1938, much expansion followed. The white area in the center of this 1950 diagram indicates the former location of the Fourteenth Street ferry terminal. (Hagley Museum and Library.)

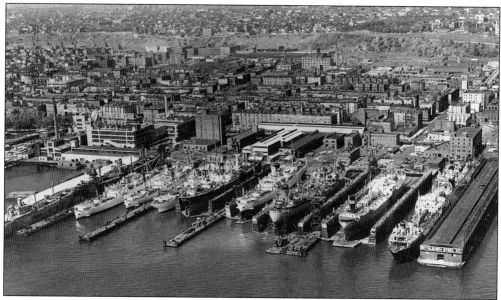

This aerial view of Hoboken's northern waterfront shows the Bethlehem Steel dry-dock facilities and piers at peak capacity. General Food's Maxwell House Coffee Plant, seen to the left, was established in Hoboken in 1938. Only an aerial view could possibly encompass the vast size of the vessels in this view. (Hagley Museum and Library.)

Seven

OF MONUMENTS AND MEMORIES

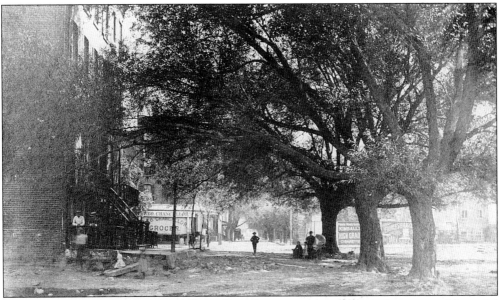

The ways in which the memories of people and times past are preserved are many. Memorial buildings can evoke the memories of those who have gone before, as can the written word paintings and sculptures. The 19th century gave us perhaps the most penetrating means of fixing a moment in time with the art of photography. This brief chapter makes mention of singular contributions to the noble work of preserving memory. This intriguing photograph not only gives us a perspective down a Hoboken street, but also, through its contrasts of dark and light, youth and age, it speaks to the passage of time. (Willenborg Family Collection, courtesy *Hoboken Almanac*, copyright Benedict J. Fernandez.)

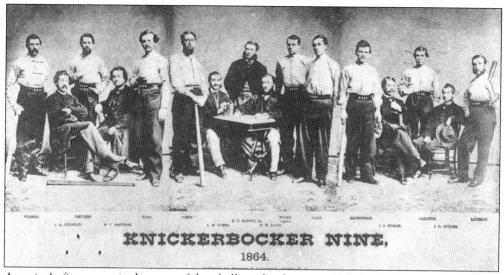

KNICKERBOCKER NINE,

1864.

America's first organized game of baseball took place on Hoboken's Elysian Fields near Eleventh Street on June 19, 1846, between the Knickerbockers and the New York Nine, using rules developed by Alexander Cartwright Jr. This is a reproduction of a photograph of the Knickerbocker Nine Baseball Club in 1864. (Courtesy Hoboken Public Library.)

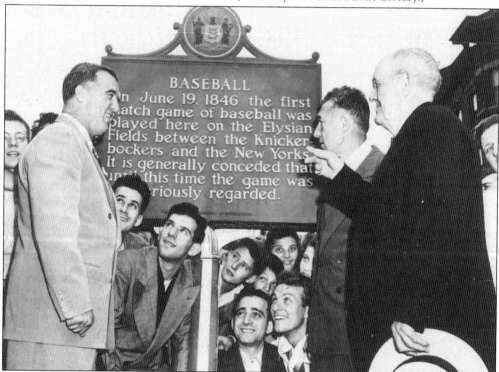

Hoboken commemorated the Baseball Centennial in 1946, with a series of festivities and a game re-enactment. Baseball Czar Albert Chadler is pictured here to the left of the commemorative plaque on Eleventh Street, with Ford Frick and Jocko Fields. At age 82, he was said to be the oldest living person who played on the original field. (Courtesy Hoboken Public Library.)

This impressive WW I bronze monument of two soldiers was unveiled and dedicated on Memorial Day, 1922. It is located in the center of Elysian Park, between Tenth and Eleventh Streets, at the foot of Castle Point Terrace, in a park given to the city by the Hoboken Land and Improvement Company.

A boulder, originally placed at the foot of Second Street at River Street by the Knights of Columbus on May 30, 1925, honors "the valiant American expeditionary forces who embarked from this port to participate in WW I 1917–1918." (Author's photograph.)

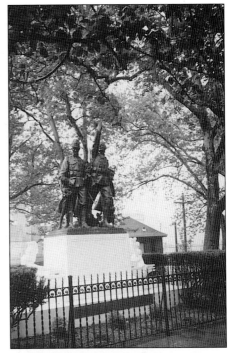

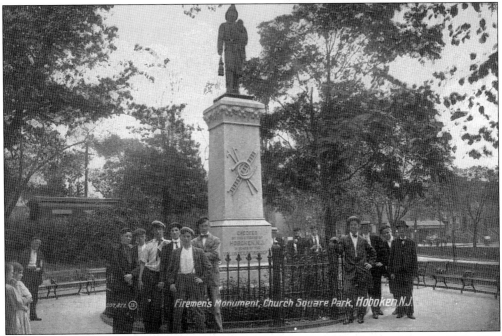

This iron monument to the Exempt Volunteer Firemen was unveiled on May 30, 1891. The firefighters of Hoboken have a long history, now being preserved in the Fire Department Museum at 215 Bloomfield Street. The seven remaining firehouses and this monument are listed on the National Register of Historic Places. Church Square Park also features a statue donated by John Minervini of Guglielmo Marconi, the Italian-born "father of the wireless." (Author's collection.)

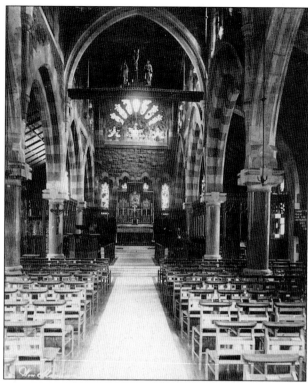

In building this living memorial to her child, Julia Augusta, Martha Bayard Stevens gave Hoboken one of its most beautiful buildings. The Episcopal Church of the Holy Innocents, listed on the National Register of Historic Places, includes a parsonage (1888) and impressive parish house (1885), designed by William Halsey Wood. The church, designed by Edward T. Potter (with an enlargement by Henry Vaughn), was consecrated on August 24, 1874. (Courtesy Hoboken Public Library.)

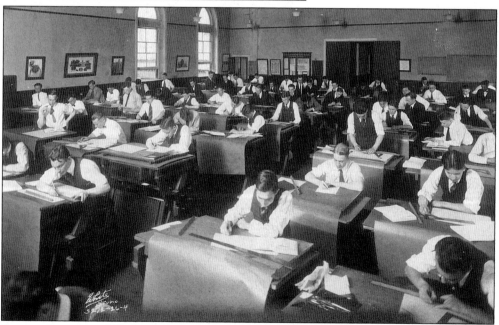

Stevens Institute of Technology was founded by Edwin Augustus Stevens in 1871. The achievements of the Stevens family and its unique involvement with the town, which Colonel John Stevens developed many years ago, are preserved in the lasting presence of this innovative technical community. This is a view of a drafting class at Stevens Institute of Technology from the 1920s. (Samuel Williams Library, Stevens Institute of Technology.)

Hoboken's Hudson County Park was designed by the noted landscape architect Charles Nassau Lowrie in the early 1900s. It was later renamed Columbus Park and features a sculpture of Christopher Columbus. (Frances Loeb Library, Harvard University.)

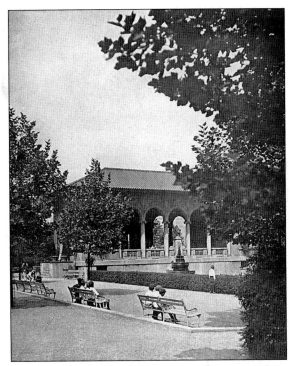

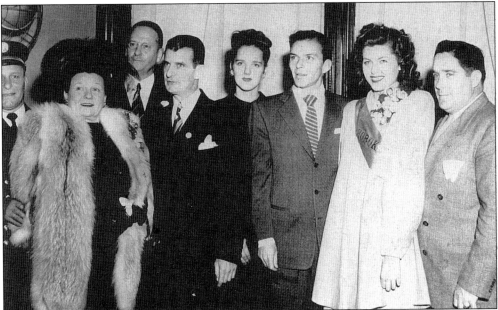

Frank Sinatra, the legendary singer, actor, and entertainer, was born in Hoboken at 415 Monroe Street. The site of his birthplace has been marked with a bronze sidewalk star. The former Shore Drive as well as a substantial pier pavilion have also been named in his honor. This photograph was taken in the mayor's office at Hoboken City Hall on October 30, 1947, when he was given the key to the city. His proud parents are to the left, Fire Captain Anthony M. (Marty) Sinatra and Natalie D. (Dolly) Sinatra. From the left in the foreground are Mayor Carmine DeSapio, Frank Sinatra, "Miss Hoboken," and Patrolman George Fitzpatrick. (Courtesy Patricia Politis.)

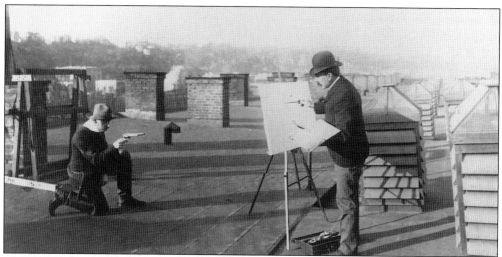

Charles Schreyvogel, whose depictions of cavalrymen and Native Americans of the southwest in oil paintings and bronzes are highly regarded, lived in Hoboken for most of his life. He is seen here painting another Hoboken resident, the Stevens Institute student Storie Schultze, on the roof of his home at 1232 Garden Street. The rugged appearance of the Palisades, seen in the background, and the quality of light recalled his visits to the southwest. (National Cowboy Hall of Fame and Western Heritage Center, Center for the study of the Western Experience.)

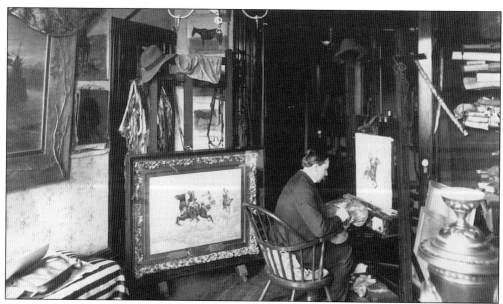

Schreyvogel's painting *My Bunkie*, now in the collection of the Metropolitan Museum of Art, won the coveted Clark Award in 1900. It is seen here on the easel in the foreground. The artist did not wish to sell it during his lifetime. He was the subject of a 1969 book by James D. Horan entitled *The Life and Work of Charles Schreyvogel: Painter-Historian of the Indian-Fighting Army of the American West*. (National Cowboy Hall of Fame and Western Heritage Center, Center for the Study of the Western Experience.)

This tintype is of a young Alfred Stieglitz, and father Edward, in a playful moment. The Stieglitz family resided on Garden Street until 1871, when Mr. Stieglitz, a Civil War veteran and merchant, moved the family to Manhattan. A.T Stewart and Marshall Field were among his major customers. (Yale University Collection of American Literature, Beineke Rare Book and Manuscript Library.)

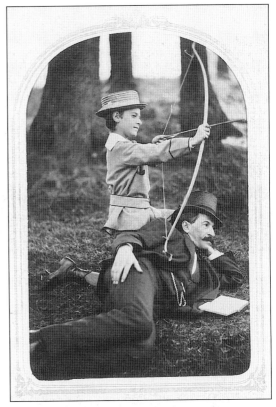

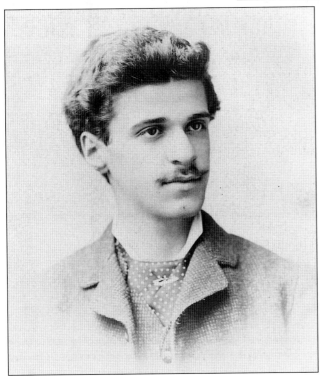

This portrait of Alfred Stieglitz as a young man reveals a determined intensity. Stieglitz, who fundamentally changed American and world photography, referred to his experiences growing up in Hoboken in the following statement accompanying an exhibit of his work from 1886 to 1921: ". . . The Exhibition is photographic throughout. My teachers have been life—work—continuous experiment . . . I was born in Hoboken. I am an American. Photography is my passion. The search for Truth my obsession." (Yale University Collection of American Literature, Beineke Rare Book and Manuscript Library.)

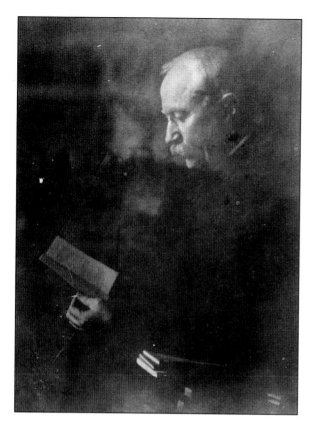

This profile portrait of Thomas F. Hatfield, librarian of the Hoboken Free Public Library, is the work of the Hoboken-born photographer Dorothea Lange. Lange traveled throughout the American West for the Farm Security Administration, creating a legacy of moving images. Mr. Hatfield was librarian from 1890 to 1924. The public library, opposite Church Square Park, is one of Hoboken's greatest resources. (Courtesy Hoboken Public Library.)

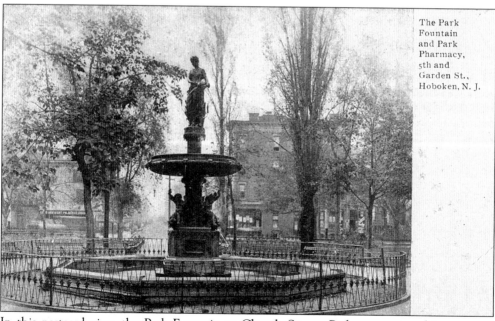

The Park Fountain and Park Pharmacy, 5th and Garden St., Hoboken, N. J.

In this postcard view, the Park Fountain at Church Square Park was captured in a serene moment. (Author's collection.)